# REEL INEQUALITY

# REEL INEQUALITY

## *Hollywood Actors and Racism*

NANCY WANG YUEN

RUTGERS UNIVERSITY PRESS
NEW BRUNSWICK, NEW JERSEY, AND LONDON

Second Printing, 2018

Library of Congress Cataloging-in-Publication Data

Names: Yuen, Nancy Wang, 1976– author.
Title: Reel inequality : Hollywood actors and racism / Nancy Wang Yuen.
Description: New Brunswick, New Jersey : Rutgers University Press, 2016. | Includes bibliographical references and index.
Identifiers: LCCN 2016012315| ISBN 9780813586304 (hardcover : alk. paper) | ISBN 9780813586298 (pbk. : alk. paper) | ISBN 9780813586311 (e-book (epub)) | ISBN 9780813586328 (e-book (web pdf))
Subjects: LCSH: Minorities in the motion picture industry—United States. | Motion picture industry—United States—Employees. | Race discrimination—United States. | Discrimination in employment—United States.
Classification: LCC PN1995.9.M56 Y83 2016 | DDC 791.43089/96073—dc23
LC record available at https://lccn.loc.gov/2016012315

A British Cataloging-in-Publication record for this book is available from the British Library.



Visit our website: www.rutgersuniversitypress.org

Manufactured in the United States of America

*For Spencer, Tabitha, and Eden*

# CONTENTS

# ACKNOWLEDGMENTS

As the first in my family to earn a doctorate and to write a book, I am indebted to the artists, mentors, friends and family who sustained me through sixteen years of research and writing. I began my research in 2000 at a panethnic theater in Southern California. The vibrant young artists of color embraced me and told me about their adventures in racist Hollywood. I am grateful to them and all of the actors and industry personnel who generously imparted me with their stories. Special thanks to Philip W. Chung and Clyde Kusatsu for sharing their industry knowledge and contacts.

My UCLA advisors were the first to read, encourage, and critique my research. When I doubted whether anyone in academia cared about Hollywood actors, Bob Emerson wisely explained the built-in popular interest in my work. Steve Clayman's kindness sustained me through grad school and beyond. He and John Heritage took a chance on me as a research assistant and taught me how to analyze media data. Min Zhou, whose mentorship began in my undergraduate years, opened doors for me to pursue a PhD in sociology and to publish my earliest research on Asian American actors. Rebecca Emigh's dedication, investment, and love made me a sociologist. Darnell Hunt's training in content analysis, ongoing mentorship, and research shaped me into a media scholar.

Book writing and publishing is a complex process fraught with mystery, heartache, elation and fatigue. I am deeply indebted to my friends Gilda Ochoa, Hung Thai, Faustina DuCros, Leisy Abrego, Christina Sue, Noriko Milman, Christina Chin, Shelley Garcia, Chinyere Osuji, Arpi Miller, Zulema Valdez, David Cook, Anthony Ocampo, Maria Su Wang, Susan Lim, Jenny Lee, Timothy Clark, Sarah Liu, Rebecca Hong, Esther Chung-Kim, and Jane Hong, for reading drafts, mentoring me, and keeping me accountable throughout the long journey. Thanks to Jooyoung Lee for suggesting the cover design. Thanks to my Biola colleagues and students (present and former)—Brad Christerson, Deshonna Collier-Goubil, Stephanie Chan, LaDawn Prieto Johnson, Cassandra Van Zandt, Carlos Delgado, Diana Rongavilla, Janelle Paule and many others for wishing me success. I also appreciate Eugene Hung, Linda Bugge Perez, Mandy Robles, Julie Nievas-Barajas, Jason Chung, Lisa Cortez, Katie Liddicoat, Gil Gonzalez, Amber Janeczek, Kelli Clifton, Heidi Beltran Santillan, Nadina De Souza and all of my friends for cheering me on and assuring me that my work has significance beyond academia.

Thanks to the editors and copy editors I worked with—Jenny Gavacs, Jude Berman, Pam Suwinsky, and, most of all, Leslie Mitchner—who believed in my book. Thanks to the entire Rutgers University Press team for making this book happen. I also appreciate the anonymous readers whose comments improved my writing and whose critiques helped me develop a thicker skin. Deepest thanks to my research assistants, Steven Morrow and Karissa Yaw, for their data coding and graphic support. I am also grateful to the National Science Foundation and UCLA for funding my early research, and to Biola University for the grant and sabbatical that made my writing possible.

My family has been my lifeline. They gave me the gift of time and support. Thanks to my sisters Allyson Wang and, especially Mallory Wang for helping me promote my book to the social media generation. I am very grateful for my parents-in-law, Amy and David Yuen, for watching my children regularly—giving me time to write. I also appreciate my children for playing and reading while I wrote, and putting up with Mommy's "Just let me finish this paragraph" mantra. I especially appreciate the times Eden managed to get my attention with her sweet persistence to give me work/life balance. Tabitha's desire to "write a book" (on my laptop whenever she saw me working on it) showed me how this book can inspire girls of color to write their own. Most of all, I am thankful for Spencer, whose love, faith, and patience got me through the daily grind and agonizing lows. Thank you for running our household daily—from dishes to laundry to making the kids lunches and breakfasts. Your sacrifice in the mundane gave my work wings. I am eternally grateful.

I grew up with very few books and a dearth of emotional and intellectual support. I could not have come this far without the grace and love of God. This book is not just the culmination of years of research but a lifetime of growth. I pray that it will open eyes to injustice, inscribe in hearts compassion and inspire minds to change.

# REEL INEQUALITY

# INTRODUCTION

> *#OscarsSoWhite . . . Again. . . . I will not be attending the Oscar ceremony this coming February. We cannot support it. . . . How is it possible for the 2nd consecutive year all 20 contenders under the actor category are white? And let's not even get into the other branches. 40 white actors in 2 years and no flava at all. We can't act?! WTF!!*
>
> —Spike Lee

In 2016, for the second consecutive year, the Academy of Motion Picture Arts and Sciences nominated white actors for all acting awards. This revived the hashtag #OscarsSoWhite, pulling back the curtain on Hollywood's enduring race problem.[1] Despite showing talent, resilience, and bankability, why do actors of color continue to lag white actors in numbers and prominence? At the epicenter is the industry's racial and gender homogeneity, epitomized by the Academy's corps of invited-only members. With a 93 percent white and 76 percent male membership,[2] the Academy has come under pressure to diversify. In protest, Spike Lee and Jada Pinkett Smith both announced they would not attend the Oscars ceremony.[3] The Academy's president, Cheryl Boone Isaacs, responded quickly with promises of change. Several (white) Academy members defended the status quo. Oscar nominee Charlotte Rampling called the protest "racist to whites" and suggested that perhaps "black actors did not deserve to make the final list."[4] Similarly, double-Oscar-winner Michael Caine said, "In the end, you can't vote for an actor because he's black. You can't say, 'I'm going to vote for him. He's not very good, but he's black.'"[5] Cries of reverse racism and blaming actors of color for their own marginalization are commonplace in Hollywood. These arguments falsely assume an equal playing field while dismissing institutional racial biases that privilege white actors for roles and recognition.

Hollywood's systemic exclusion of actors of color is evident in the Academy's abysmal record of nominating and awarding actors of color. In Oscar's eighty-eight-year history, actors of color received only 6.2 percent of total acting nominations and won only 7.8 percent of total acting awards (see fig. 1). The only woman of color to ever win a best actress award was African American actor Halle Berry in 2002 for her performance in *Monster's Ball.* Fifty-nine years have passed since the last (and only) Asian female actor won an acting Oscar (Miyoshi Umeki, 1957 best supporting actress for her performance in *Sayonara*) and twenty-five years since a Latina took home an acting Oscar (Mercedes Ruehl, 1991 best supporting actress for her performance in *The Fisher King*). No acting Oscar has gone to an actor of Asian, Latina/o, or indigenous descent for the past fifteen years. By deeming only white actors worth honoring, the Academy reproduces Hollywood's structural racial bias.

Though public pressures have prompted the Academy to implement immediate changes to diversify its membership,[6] the impact on future nominations remains uncertain. This is because the

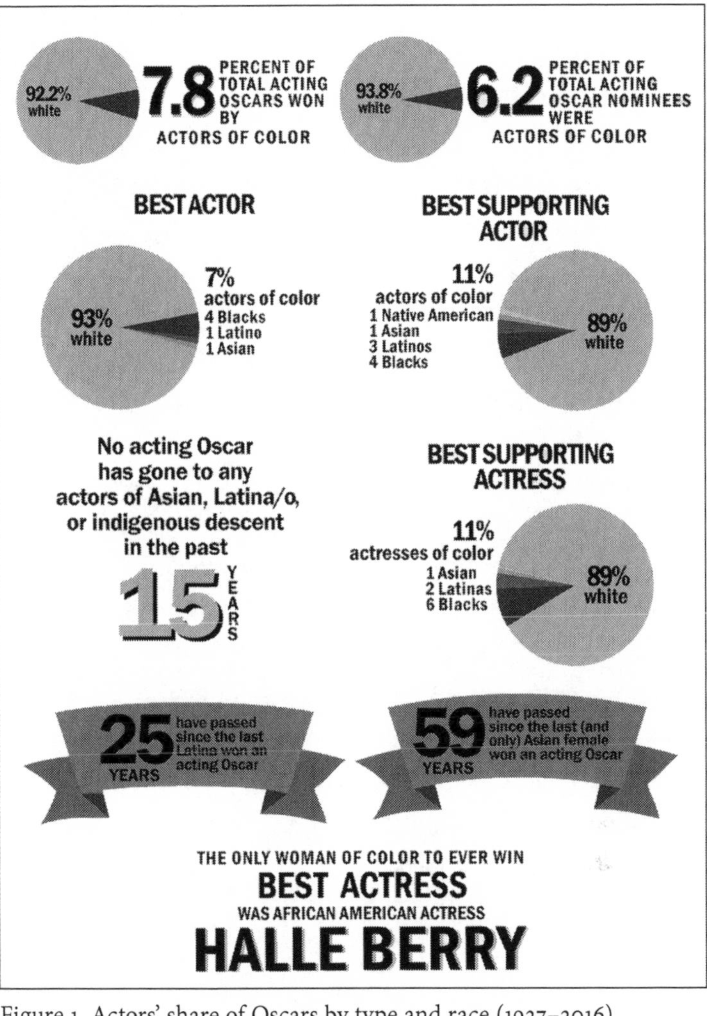


Figure 1. Actors' share of Oscars by type and race (1927–2016)
*Note*: For the four acting categories (Best Actor, Best Actress, Best Supporting Actor, and Best Supporting Actress), total Oscar winners numbered 336 while total acting nominations numbered 1,667.
*Sources*: Designed by Karissa Yaw. Data from Academy of Motion Picture Arts and Sciences, "The Official Academy Awards® Database," http://awardsdatabase.oscars.org/ampas_awards/BasicSearchInput.jsp; Susan King, "Oscar Diversity: It's Been 54 Years since a Latina Took Home an Academy Award," *Los Angeles Times*, January 21, 2016, http://www.latimes.com/entertainment/movies/la-et-mn-oscar-diversity-asian-latino-indigenous-nominees-winners-20160120-story.html; Ana Maria Benedetti, "A Look Back at the Lack of Latinos in Oscar History," *Huffpost Latino Voices*, February 20, 2015, http://www.huffingtonpost.com/2015/02/20/latino-oscar-history_n_6723284.html.

Academy's diversity problem is not just numerical but also ideological. The Academy constrains actors of color by granting Oscars to a narrow set of stereotyped roles. David Oyelowo describes how black actors "have been celebrated more for when we are subservient . . . not just in the Academy, but in life generally. We have been slaves, we have been domestic servants, we have been criminals, we have been all of those things. But we have been leaders, we have been kings, we have been those who changed the world."[7] Hattie McDaniel, the first African American actor to win an Academy Award (best supporting actress in 1940), played house slave Mammy in *Gone with the Wind* (1939). More than seventy years later, Academy Award winners of color still play servile roles. Octavia Spencer won the 2012 best supporting actress award for playing a maid in *The Help*, and Lupita Nyong'o won the 2014 best supporting actress award for playing a slave in *12 Years a Slave*. Producer Ice Cube, in discussing *Straight Outta Compton*'s 2016 Oscar snubs, joked, "Maybe we should've put a slave in *Straight Outta Compton*. I think that's where we messed up . . . just one random slave for the Academy members to recognize us as a real, black movie."[8]

Though actors of color have played leaders, they rarely win Oscars for such roles. Denzel Washington won the best actor Oscar for playing a corrupt cop in *Training Day* (2001), but not for his widely lauded performance of the title character in *Malcom X* (1992). Another noteworthy performance, David Oyelowo's critically acclaimed portrayal of Martin Luther King Jr. in *Selma* (2014), did not even garner a nomination. By honoring actors of color for playing slaves, maids, and criminals rather than civil rights leaders, the Academy denies them the full breadth of accolades afforded to white actors. The Academy may or may not intentionally vote for roles that keep people of color "in their place," but its record reveals a pattern of bias. Consequently, the Academy will have to diversify more than just members' numbers, but their hearts and minds, as well.

#OscarsSoWhite is a symptom of Hollywood's larger race problem. The exclusion and stereotyping of actors of color extend far beyond the Academy Awards. Even though people of color made up 37.4 percent of the US population in 2013, actors of color played only 6.5 percent of lead roles in broadcast television shows and 16.7 percent of lead roles in films.[9] Furthermore, Hollywood tends to view actors of color—from the Oscar contenders to the average working actor—through a racist lens, reducing them to tokens and caricatures. Hiro,[10] a veteran Japanese American working actor in his late sixties, told me that Hollywood never sees him beyond his race. When he was a guest star on a television show, the white male director continually referred to him as an "Asian actor in this part," but described another white male guest star as a "good killer" and "gushed" about his "wonderful [acting] moments." For white actors, race is a privilege rather than a reduction. From *Iron Man* to *Mad Men,* white men access a dazzling array of lead roles in nearly every genre and medium. In my interviews, several white male actors confessed to having a racial advantage. Roane, a white male actor in his mid-twenties, said, "I'm very lucky. There are a lot of roles for young, white kids. I've got buddies who are Puerto Rican or African American, and they have a hard time finding work."

This book is about how actors of color experience racism in the Hollywood industry, which I define as the system of major and minor film and television studios along with the production companies they fund.[11] Although the current Hollywood industry is less centralized than the earliest studio system, racial barriers continue to persist, even if they have diminished somewhat over the years. Roles have increased for actors of color, but most groups have yet to achieve US population parity. Even as more actors of color star in their own shows and films, most continue to play supporting and bit parts. From talent agent offices to film sets, actors of color still face stereotypes that bar them from reaching their full artistic potential. The persistent exclusion and stereotyping of actors of color for the past century demonstrate how far we are from a postracial society; that is, a society in which racism no longer exists. At the same time, actors of color demonstrate resilience as they creatively challenge stereotypes in their auditions and performances. A growing number of performers of color create original Web series, some of which cross over into mainstream Hollywood. So while Hollywood still represents race in problematic ways, actors of color are performing counter-takes informed by their own identities and experiences. Taking readers behind the scenes, this book reveals how actors of color suffer and survive in spite of the odds.

## Effects of Media Stereotypes

Growing up as an immigrant kid in Southern California, just miles from the Hollywood industry, I watched hours of television for amusement. This continues to be the norm today. In 2015, the average US resident consumed "traditional and digital media for over 1.7 trillion hours, an average of approximately 15 and-a-half hours per person per day."[12] In the same year, children (eight- to twelve-year-olds) consumed an average of six hours of media a day, and teens consumed nine hours.[13] This mindboggling amount of media consumption shapes how we see the world we live in. Even though my neighborhood was racially and ethnically diverse when I was growing up, the world looked completely white on television. I absorbed a very narrow vision of US culture. All throughout my childhood, I did not see myself represented in film and television beyond the occasional cringe-worthy Asian nerd or massage parlor worker. In the film and television worlds, only white lives mattered, and the rest of us were either marginalized or demonized. In college, where I learned that race is not biological but socially constructed, I also saw how Hollywood dramatized racial differences as natural and fixed. Far from neutral, mass media institutions such as Hollywood are major transmitters of racist ideologies. Antonio Gramsci theorized that society's elites use the mass media to maintain "hegemony," or the dominance one social group holds over others.[14] Hollywood's dominant narratives of whites as heroes and actors of color as sidekicks or villains legitimate and reproduce the racial hierarchies existent in US society.

Though they are largely fictional, on-screen images can shape our views of reality. I witnessed this firsthand when I went to see *Skyfall* (2012), a James Bond film. Preview after preview of action films featured white male protagonists shooting and killing people, yet it was the preview for *Django Unchained* (2012) that elicited an extreme audience reaction. In one scene, Django (played by Jamie Foxx), a black slave-turned-bounty-hunter, says, "Kill white folks, and they pay you for it—what's not to like?" This statement caused two middle-aged white women sitting in my row to groan loudly, as one of them griped, "That's what's wrong with our urban areas!" Even though we were about to watch a violent James Bond film and had just sat through brutal violence enacted by Tom Cruise, Bruce Willis, and Arnold Schwarzenegger, none of those previews elicited critique. The lack of black heroes in film and television, coupled with the preponderance of white heroes and black villains, demonizes black male violence and legitimizes white male violence. Furthermore, this extrapolation of a fictional Django to "our urban areas" demonstrates how audiences fail to distinguish between fiction and reality in racial stereotypes. Through countless reiterations in popular media, racial stereotypes can become *real* in the minds of audiences.[15]

Popular media can have a negative impact on whites' perceptions of people of color. One study found that nonverbal racial biases in facial expressions and body language, as represented on popular television shows, influence white viewers' racial biases.[16] Furthermore, a lack of contact between racial groups can lead to greater reliance on media stereotypes when formulating ideas about people outside one's race.[17] Studies show that audiences substitute stereotypes they see on screen for reality when they have not had any direct interactions with particular racial groups.[18] For instance, Latino stereotypes in the media can lead audiences negatively to associate immigration with increased unemployment and crime.[19] Film and television can also exacerbate preexisting racist fears. For example, people who perceive that they live in a neighborhood with a high percentage of blacks are more likely than those who do not hold that perception to fear crime after watching scripted crime dramas.[20]

Given that whites greatly overestimate the share of crimes committed by blacks,[21] media stereotypes can aggravate such misperceptions and can be used to justify violence against people of color. Darren Wilson—the white police officer who shot and killed Michael Brown, an unarmed black man, in Ferguson, Missouri—characterized Brown as a "demon" and a "hulk." Journalists pointed out that Wilson's descriptors came from the "black brute" racial stereotype, a "stock figure of white supremacist rhetoric in the lynching era of the late 19th and early 20th centuries,"[22] as popularized in Hollywood films.[23] Furthermore, the media's tendency to fuel racial misperceptions can contribute to the disparate punishment of people of color.[24] Film and television can also cultivate existent fears of foreign threat. In 2014, a journalist critiqued the popular cable television show *Homeland* as perpetuating Middle Eastern stereotypes used to "justify actions in the real world—U.S. wars, covert operations and drone strikes; CIA detention and torture; racist policing, domestic surveillance and militarized borders."[25] Racism, when packaged as entertainment, can skew the way viewers understand and categorize people.

In addition to aggravating racial tensions, the erasure and negative portrayals of people of color can adversely affect how people of color see themselves. Prolonged television exposure predicts a decrease in self-esteem for all girls and for black boys, and an increase in self-esteem for white boys.[26] These differences correlate with the racial and gender biases in Hollywood, which casts only white men as heroes, while erasing or subordinating other groups as villains, sidekicks, and sexual objects. Studies also show how media images of Native American mascots lower the self-esteem and affect the moods of Native American adolescents and young adults, who have the highest suicide rates in the United States.[27] The ubiquity of racist imagery can have cumulative effects on society. We cannot dismiss the media's differential portrayals of racial groups as mere entertainment if we are to take seriously their impact on our youth.

## A Brief History of Hollywood's Racism

Racism, in the form of job exclusion and racially stereotyped roles, has defined the Hollywood film industry since its birth in the early 1900s. The first characters of color were portrayed as morally and intellectually deficient by white actors in blackface, brownface, and yellowface—makeup used to portray characters of a different race. The practice of white actors playing characters of color came from minstrel shows, popularized in the United States in the 1830s and 1840s.[28] The early performers were mainly Irish and Jewish immigrants, who did not share equal status with earlier European immigrants (mainly of Anglo-Saxon origin) to the United States.[29] Through their performances, the Irish and Jewish minstrels "whitened themselves" by promoting white ethnic behaviors as acceptable, while denouncing behaviors by blacks, Native Americans and Chinese as abnormal and criminal.[30] Minstrelsy on stage and screen was a widespread form of entertainment and helped the Irish and Jews assimilate into white culture and status.[31] In fact, Jewish studio magnates in the 1920s and 1930s purposefully "presented a Hollywood version of Jewishness that was just as white and equally 'American,'" focusing on virtues of hard work, sacrifice, and family values.[32] Many white ethnic actors achieved stardom (and assimilation) in the 1940s and 1950s by dropping their ethnic names: Doris Kapplehoff became Doris Day and Dino Crocetti became Dean Martin.[33] In contrast, Hollywood's systemic discrimination prevented actors of color from achieving stardom. James Shigeta, a Japanese American actor whose work in Hollywood began in the late 1950s, recalled a musical film producer telling him, "If you were white, you'd be a hell of a big star."[34] Although race can change over time for some groups (as demonstrated by the "whitening" of the Irish and Jews), the majority of African Americans, Asian Americans, Latina/os, and Native Americans continue to experience race (and racism) as paramount over other identifiers.[35]

Hollywood's early films drew on the legacy of minstrelsy, presenting people of color as comedic buffoons or lecherous villains. From the blackface portrayals of African Americans as fools, rapists, and schemers in D. W. Griffith's *The Birth of a Nation* (1915) to the yellowface performances of Asians as diabolical, inscrutable, and exotic foreigners, Hollywood has a rich history of casting white actors to mock people of color. The brownface portrayals of Latinos as *banditos* (or violent and immoral criminals), starting with the silent "greaser" films in the 1910s,[36] became so egregious that the Mexican government banned such films in early 1922.[37] The Mexican government lifted the ban on November 6, 1922, after the Motion Picture Producers and Distributors of America (MPPDA)[38] agreed to stop making films offensive to Mexico or any other Latin American country. However, the Hollywood studios got around this agreement by inventing fake Latin American countries, such as Orinomo and San Benito, to recycle the same offensive stereotypes.[39]

When actors of color did appear on screen in the twentieth century, they were mainly background characters, stereotypes, and occasional foils to white leads. Roles for women of color were extremely rare and were played mostly by white women. Luise Rainer played the lead Chinese female character in *The Good Earth* (1937), Katharine Hepburn played the lead Chinese female character in *Dragon Seed* (1944), and Natalie Wood played the lead Puerto Rican female character in *West Side Story* (1961).[40] The few notable exceptions were all men of color: Sessue Hayakawa (Japanese American) and Ramón Novarro (Mexican American) were matinee idols in the 1910s and 1920s, and Anthony Quinn (Oscar-winning Mexican American) and Sidney Poitier (Oscar-winning African American) were film stars in the 1950s and 1960s.[41] Despite achieving rare stardom, these actors of color still faced stereotyped roles.

Institutionally, Hollywood excluded actors of color from equal employment access through its production codes. From 1930 to 1956, Hollywood formally barred actors of color from most film leads through an anti-miscegenation clause that banned depictions of interracial relationships.[42] This clause was part of Hollywood's self-imposed censorship regulations (called the Motion Picture Production Code, or Hays code), and mirrored anti-miscegenation laws that criminalized marriage and intimate relationships between white persons and any persons of color. Because actors of color were not allowed to star in a relationship with a white actor (even if the white actor was playing a character of color), they were systematically excluded from lead roles. The Hays code prevented Chinese American actor Anna May Wong from being cast as O-lan, the Chinese female lead in *The Good Earth* (1937), opposite a white actor cast to play the Chinese male lead.[43] Instead, Luise Rainer (a white actor) was cast to play O-lan—winning a best actress Oscar for her performance. Given the scarcity of stories about people of color, the casting of white actors as leads of color prevented actors of color from achieving stardom.

Throughout the years, Hollywood also bypassed equal employment laws. In March 1969, the Equal Employment Opportunity Commission (EEOC) held a one-day hearing in Hollywood to address the "clear evidence of a pattern or practice of discrimination in violation of Title VII of the Civil Rights Act of 1964" in the film industry.[44] They presented evidence that people of color were excluded from nearly all jobs in Hollywood except the lowest-paying and lowest-skill jobs.[45] In response, the Justice Department prepared lawsuits against six of the seven major motion picture studios, the Association of Motion Picture and Television Producers (AMPTP), and the International Alliance of Theatrical State Employees (IATSE) to address the "gross underutilization" of racial minority workers in major positions of talent and production.[46] However, the film studios successfully lobbied and campaigned against this intervention, solidifying white domination in the industry to this day.

Hollywood producers also use the protection of the First Amendment to bypass nondiscriminatory hiring laws. Requests for particular racial and gender categories in casting notices (or job advertisements for actors) should violate Title VII of the Civil Rights Act of 1964, which protects minorities from discrimination.

However, producers can hire actors based on specific racial, gender, and age categories by simply claiming that the categories serve the story they want to tell. Using "freedom of speech" to defend all casting decisions, Hollywood continues to discriminate against actors of color with legal impunity. Most industry contracts and codes even have a clause that protects producers' "exclusive creative prerogatives" in casting.[47] Actors also fear getting blacklisted if they report racial discrimination. In fact, no court has ever made a formal judgment or decision about an actor's claim of race or gender discrimination in job advertisements.[48]

With a history of exclusion and no legal protection, actors of color continue to face stunted opportunities in mainstream film and television. For example, in 1999, no actor of color had a lead role on any of the twenty-six new shows premiering on the major broadcast television networks.[49] More than a decade later, change has been minimal. Despite an increased number of broadcast television shows featuring actors of color in the 2014–2015 prime-time season, the overall season still saw white actors playing show regulars at a rate nearly 10 percent greater than their percentage of the US population.[50] Even though people of color comprised 37.4 percent of the US population and purchased 44 percent of domestically sold tickets in 2014,[51] actors of color played only a quarter of the speaking characters in the top one hundred films.[52] These discrepancies demonstrate systemic barriers that prevent actors of color from accessing the same opportunities as white actors.

Exacerbating these low numbers is the continued casting of whites as characters of color, which reduces the number of leads for actors of color. White actors played the Latino leads in films such as *Casa de Mi Padre* (2012) and *Argo* (2012), the African American leads in *A Mighty Heart* (2007) and *Stuck* (2007), the Asian leads in *Aloha* (2015) and *Ghost in the Shell* (2017), Native American characters in films such as *Pan* (2015) and *The Lone Ranger* (2013), and the Egyptian leads in *Exodus: Gods and Kings* (2014).[53] In 2016, for example, two white English actors were cast as men of color in forthcoming films: Charlie Hunnam to play a Mexican American drug lord in *American Drug Lord* and Joseph Fiennes to play black pop icon Michael Jackson in a "9/11 road-trip drama."[54] Even when critiqued, Hollywood executives and directors defend such castings. In response to criticisms of *Exodus*'s casting, media mogul Rupert Murdoch tweeted, "Since when are Egyptians not white? All I know are."[55] Similarly, when asked why he cast himself (a white male) and not a Latino to play the Latino lead (based on real life CIA officer, Tony Mendez) in *Argo* (2012), Ben Affleck answered, "Tony does not have, I don't know what you would say, a Latin/Spanish accent," and "You wouldn't necessarily select him out of a line of 10 people and go, 'This guy's Latino.'"[56] Affleck basically stated that Latino actors should only play accented roles. This is part of a larger industry perception that actors of color are only fit to play a limited, often stereotyped set of roles. Hollywood continues to cast white actors to portray the range of humanity, while barring qualified actors of color from portraying people of color.

In an ideal Hollywood industry, all actors can play all ethnicities equally. After all, acting is pretending to be someone else. However, Hollywood is not an equal playing field when actors of color remain invisible or sidelined to a select few shows while white actors enjoy the privilege to portray every role under the sun—even characters of color. Film and television shows continue to exclude talented actors of color based solely on their race. Case in point, acclaimed black British actor Idris Elba, despite being a fan favorite to play the next James Bond, has met resistance from Roger Moore (former Bond actor), who said Bond should be "English-English,"[57] and from Anthony Horowitz (the author commissioned by Ian Fleming's estate to write the next James Bond novel), who said Elba was "too 'street' for Bond."[58] These racially coded comments demonstrate the double standard actors of color face when playing crossover characters. Until Hollywood provides actors of color proportionate access to all roles (especially leads), white actors should not play characters of color. For example, white actors should not play Latina/o leads, given that none of the top ten films or network television shows in 2013 cast a single Latina/o actor in a lead role.[59] With Latinos making up 17 percent of the US population, their invisibility in Hollywood is a gross misrepresentation of the American landscape. In that same year, the Academy awarded the best picture Oscar to *Argo* (in which white actor Ben Affleck plays the Latino lead), but no acting Oscar to an actor of color. When the types of roles are unlimited for white actors, their chances of winning awards increase. This is in great contrast with actors of color, who struggle to find lead roles that showcase their talent.

## The Industry Today

Today, Hollywood is one of the biggest entertainment and media industries in the world, with its $449 billion profits exceeding those of professional sports ($23 billion), the alcohol industry ($227 billion), and the gambling industry ($37 billion).[60] Such large sums of money also bring great risk. If a film flops, a studio can lose hundreds of millions of dollars. Consequently, Hollywood relies heavily on past hits, formulas, and big-name actors. This institutional risk aversion goes hand in hand with racial bias. Within this system, actors of color are often caught in a vicious cycle, wherein they have few opportunities to become bankable stars, making them financial risks, which in turn limits their role prospects and prominence.

In chapter 1, I review the severe racial imbalance experienced by professional actors and behind-the-scenes creative talent and executives. Drawing on industry statistics and interviews conducted with professional actors and other industry personnel in the industry, I argue that a set of predominantly white male creative talent, business executives, and gatekeepers breeds a culture of ethnocentric storytelling and casting. The industry maintains the racial status quo by invoking colorblind rationales that attribute white male dominance to individualistic merit and cultural explanations. In chapter 2, I demystify common colorblind rationales used within Hollywood to justify racist hiring practices while maintaining a facade of progressive openness. By blaming racial inequality on a lack of talent, market forces, and creative prerogative, Hollywood denies its culpability in reproducing structural racism.

There are approximately 63,230 professional actors working in the United States.[61] The average member of the actors' union earns $52,000 a year,[62] while 95 percent make less than $100,000 annually.[63] The actors I interviewed exemplify the average member.[64] They call themselves "working," "middle-class," and "journeyman" actors. These working actors have modest and often unstable income streams. They spoke to me about their careers going through times of "feast or famine." The Screen Actors Guild–American Federation of Television and Radio Artists (SAG-AFTRA) union advises that "most professional performers generally need several potential income streams to earn enough money to sustain performing as a full-time career."[65] Not only do working actors make up the majority of the talent pool, but working actors also populate the supporting and background roles, most of which are one-dimensional. Furthermore, they have to audition for all of their work, rather than being offered roles by studios. Dick, a forty-five-year-old white male actor, describes the different expectations directors have for "stars" versus working actors: "The stars have the luxury of actually being able to experiment and try stuff and have that creative relationship with the director. But, with workhorses like myself, they want us to do what they paid us to do and for us not to be a headache or a question mark." Hollywood expects little to no deviance in performances from working actors. But those expectations differ for white actors and actors of color. In chapter 3, I address racial differences in typecasting. Even though all actors experience typecasting to some extent, actors of color face additional professional and emotional constraints due to racial stereotyping. In chapter 4, I discuss the double bind Latino and Asian American actors face for not being "American" (that is, white) enough for some roles and not "ethnic" enough for other roles. The limbo they occupy reveals Hollywood's inability to cast actors of color beyond narrow stereotypes. By identifying the different forms and effects of racial stereotyping from an actor's perspective, this book provides a greater understanding of how racism permeates the entertainment industry.

Professional actors are an ideal group for studying racism in Hollywood. By examining the process of how actors of color negotiate and enact roles, this book unpacks the process of racial stereotyping in behind-the-scenes social interactions in the Hollywood industry. Furthermore, acting has long been used as a framework to understand the process by which people create and perform social roles in everyday life.[66] At every stage, professional actors are subject to judgment and evaluation to determine whether they match external expectations. Despite differences between Hollywood sets and real life, a study of professional actors can reveal aspects of identity negotiation that are opaque in other settings. Professional actors of color are self-consciously aware of racial stereotyping because they are literally asked to perform and embody stereotyped traits. As they intentionally take on false roles, actors are highly aware of the tension between role playing and their "true" identities. Actors of color describe in detail how they negotiate this tension, as their own experiences often clash with Hollywood's stereotyped expectations. To deal with this tension, actors of color develop different justifications for playing stereotypes, as documented in chapter 5. At the same time, working actors are not completely powerless, but can exert some creativity over their own performances. In chapter 6, I document how working actors of color challenge stereotypes both within and outside Hollywood. Though they are limited in power, working actors of color see themselves as activists—challenging Hollywood's racism one costume or one accent at a time. Moreover, they can turn to digital media spaces, such as YouTube, to create and star in original shows.

I wrote this book to give voice to the working actors of color whose stories of big struggles and small triumphs deserve an audience. Professional actors' experiences shed light on how people of color experience discrimination but manage to preserve their identities within racially biased environments. Although actors' stories of racism demonstrate how far we are from a postracial society, their attempts to subvert and challenge stereotypes reveal their resilience and creativity. I also wrote this book to fight for equal employment of actors of color within Hollywood. In the final chapter of the book, I suggest economic and moral imperatives for racial diversity. I also document past and current efforts to achieve equal representation of actors of color in Hollywood, while making some suggestions of my own. In appendix A, I include a list of diversity programs available to actors of color within the Hollywood industry and a list of civil rights and ethnic media organizations for readers who want to take action. My hope is that this book will expose Hollywood's systemic racism, while empowering readers to advocate on behalf of actors of color.

# 1

# HOLLYWOOD'S WHITEST

*Tonight we celebrate Hollywood's best and whitest, sorry . . . brightest.*

—Neil Patrick Harris

Oscar host Neil Patrick Harris satirized the Academy's all-white acting nominations in 2015.[1] The following year, Oscar host Chris Rock dubbed the Academy Awards as "the White People's Choice Awards."[2] However, Hollywood's white dominance is not a joke. From media ownership down to the average working actor, whites saturate the ranks. Whites are 62.6 percent of the US population but make up between 74 and 96 percent of Hollywood personnel—from professional actors to decision makers responsible for creative and casting choices.[3] White male decision makers fund projects by white men, who tend to tell stories with white male leads.[4] Nearly all of the 2016 best picture Oscar nominees told stories of white men triumphing over enormous odds.[5] By making white men the center of nearly every narrative, Hollywood films and television shows naturalize their positions of power in every institution.

Hollywood's stories, though fictional, transmit real ideologies. When film and television privilege white stories over other stories, they reinforce a racial hierarchy that devalues people of color. Not only do dramatic racial disparities indicate employment discrimination in Hollywood, the underrepresentation of people of color in film and television can also have wider societal consequences. Since the media landscape can blur reality and fiction for viewers, the erasure of actors of color on screen can skew real-life perceptions. When audiences never see actors of color in major roles, they are less likely to perceive them as on equal footing with whites. Inversely, when whites and their stories are celebrated more than their fair share, audiences begin to associate significance, admiration, and power with that group over others.

Hollywood's biased employment practices have contributed to the dominance of whites across its ranks. For instance, Hollywood's union admission policies—past and present—have perpetuated a predominantly white workforce. Historically, nepotism reigned supreme in Hollywood, allowing only relatives of existing members (the majority of whom were white) into its unions.[6] Today, unions such as the Directors Guild of America (DGA) and the Producers Guild of America (PGA) still require member endorsements and sponsorship.[7] This inevitably leads to racial insularity because white Americans have social networks that are 91 percent white.[8] As a result, Hollywood's unions remain primarily populated by white people, who recommend or refer their white friends and family. Furthermore, creative industries like Hollywood rely on social networks, resulting in a majority-white hiring pool. Even if whites in the industry do not consciously bar people of color, union policies and social networks effectively do so. To better understand the scope of white dominance in Hollywood, I examine racial disparities, both in front of and behind the camera.

## Professional Actors

In 1977, the US Commission on Civil Rights released *Window Dressing on the Set: Women and Minorities in Television*, the first report on network television's racial and gender exclusionary practices and stereotyped portrayals.[9] Little has changed in the almost four decades since this report. While people of color made up 37.4 percent of the US population in 2013, actors of color were significantly underrepresented in film and television (see fig. 2). Even in 2015, regular actors of color on broadcast prime-time television lagged 9.2 percentage points behind the corresponding US population's percentage.[10]

Actors of color fare worse in lead roles. In 2013, actors of color occupied fewer than one-fifth of cable television and film leads, and

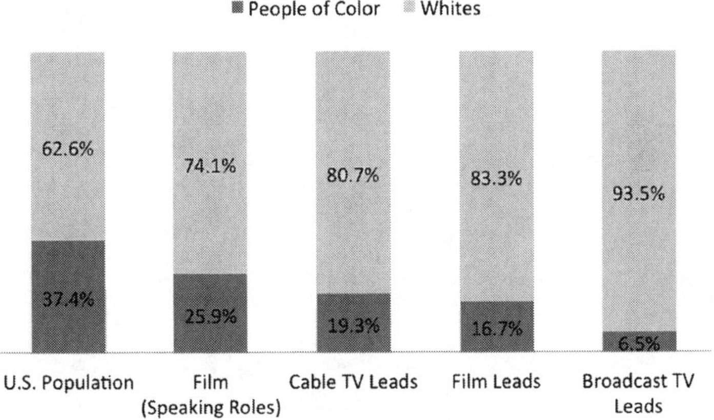


Figure 2. Actors' share of roles by type and race (2013)
*Sources*: US population (2014 estimate): US Census, "State and County Quickfacts," http://quickfacts.census.gov/qfd/states/00000.html; "Film (Speaking)" (2013): Smith, Choueiti, and Pieper, "Race/Ethnicity in 600 Popular Films: Examining on Screen Portrayals and Behind the Camera Diversity"; "Film Leads" (2011–2013), "Broadcast TV Leads" (2012–2013), and "Cable TV Leads" (2012–2013): Darnell Hunt and Ana-Christina Ramon, "2015 Hollywood Diversity Report: Flipping the Script" (Los Angeles: Ralph J. Bunche Center for African American Studies at UCLA, 2015).

fewer than one-tenth of broadcast television leads (see fig. 2). In 2014, the number of leads of color remained low, dipping even further in cable television and film.[11] Coveted lead roles typically speak the most lines, have the longest time on screen, and display the most emotional depth and complexity. Audiences are most likely to identify with leads in film and television. Given the importance of lead roles, the overrepresentation of white actors as lead characters not only gives them a professional advantage but also constructs a narrative of white supremacy.

### *African American Actors*

Compared with other groups of color, African Americans have been more visible in US popular culture. The black/white binary is fundamental to how the Americans conceptualize race and race relations given the complex racial history of the United States.[12] Consequently, since *The Birth of a Nation* (1915), African Americans have "figured prominently in Hollywood's racist symbolic relations" because of their "unique history of material and cultural oppression as well as their rich expressive resources."[13] African American actors have had more opportunities than any other nonwhite group to make the "Ulmer Hot List," a ranking list of top A-list actors.[14] The visibility of African Americans is reflected in their role shares—often at or above their 2013 percentage in the US population (see fig. 3). African Americans occupied 14 percent of both film and cable television roles in 2013. Though African Americans fell below their population percentage in the 2013–2014 television season, accounting for 10 percent of broadcast regulars, their numbers rose to 14 percent in the 2014–2015 season.[15]

Despite having a greater presence, African American actors still face limitations. A significant number of film and television shows

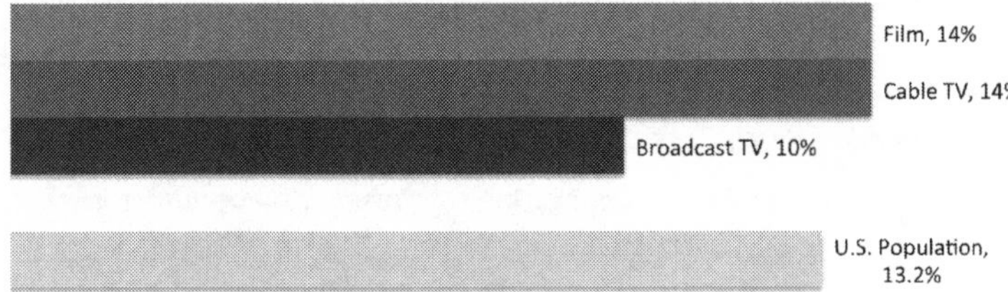


Figure 3. African American shares of roles by type (2013)
*Sources*: US Population (2014 estimate): US Census, "State and County Quickfacts," http://quickfacts.census.gov/qfd/states/00000.html; "Film (Speaking)" (2013): Smith, Choueiti, and Pieper, "Race/Ethnicity in 600 Popular Films: Examining on Screen Portrayals and Behind the Camera Diversity"; "Cable TV" and "Broadcast TV" (2012–2013): Darnell Hunt and Ana-Christina Ramon, "2015 Hollywood Diversity Report: Flipping the Script" (Los Angeles: Ralph J. Bunche Center for African American Studies at UCLA, 2015).

have no black characters.[16] In 2013, the percentage of African Americans in more than half of the top-grossing films was smaller than in the US population, while nearly a fifth of these films had no African American characters at all.[17] Similarly, 16 percent—37 percent of all cinematic, television, or streaming stories in 2014–2015 failed to portray a single speaking or named African American on screen.[18] Many African American actors find roles in all-black films and television shows, which typically have lower budgets and limited distribution.[19] Consequently, upon closer examination, even when African American actors reach population parity, they do not enjoy the same breadth of representation as white actors.

Lead roles also remain elusive for African American actors. Chris Rock wrote, "When it comes to casting, Hollywood pretty much decides to cast a black guy or they don't. We're never on the 'short list.' We're never 'in the mix.'"[20] Similarly, Will, a black male actor in his late twenties, told me about his limited opportunities compared with those of a white male actor friend:

> I have a friend. . . . We moved to New York together . . . good-looking white guy, leading man. His opportunities and my opportunities are so different. This guy gets so many opportunities, and they're leads. They're big, big leading things, so much that at the busy times of the year, he can't go in on everything. He gets so many opportunities that he's tripping over them, while I'm going in for three lines.

African American female actors experience even fewer quality lead roles because of a combination of racial and gender limitations. Hollywood is less likely to cast an African American woman opposite an African American man because the industry operates according to the myth that international audiences will not see films with black couples.[21] For example, *Hitch* (2005) intentionally cast Latina actor Eva Mendes opposite African American actor Will Smith instead of an African American woman.[22] Prior to *Scandal*'s premiere in 2012 on ABC, a black woman had not led a network television drama in nearly forty years.[23] Viola Davis described black female actors as having only "two or three categories," compared with white female actors, who have different roles for every age category.[24] Beating the odds, Viola Davis became the first African American female actor to win an "outstanding lead actress in a dramatic series" Emmy in 2015. Taraji P. Henson won the 2016 Golden Globe Award for the best actress in a television drama, the third African American female actor to do so in seventy-three years. Though African American actors still lag behind white actors in opportunities, they have made tremendous strides toward greater representation and recognition.

### *Latina/o Actors*

Compared with other groups of color, Latina/o actors have the biggest disparity between their on-screen presence and US population percentage. Despite being the largest nonwhite group in the United States (17 percent of the population), Latinas/os were severely underrepresented in film and television in 2013. Specifically, Latinas/os represented only 5 percent of film speaking roles, 3 percent of cable television regulars, and 2 percent of broadcast television regulars (see fig. 4). Latinas/os were underrepresented by a factor of more than eight to one in broadcast television. In 2014–2015, Latinas/os played only 5.8 percent of all speaking/named characters in film, TV, and streaming services.[25] Chris Rock wrote, "But forget whether Hollywood is black enough. A better question is: Is Hollywood Mexican enough? You're in L.A, you've got to *try* not to hire Mexicans."[26] Latinas/os make up 48.3 percent of Los Angeles County.[27] Blanca Valdez, who runs a Latina/o casting agency in Los Angeles, said that Latinas/os have a difficult time auditioning for roles unless the call specifically asks for "diversity" or "multiethnic"; in any case, most are secondary roles, such as a neighbor or a bank teller.[28]

US film and television have rarely cast Latina/o actors in lead roles. In 2013, no Latinas/os starred as leads in the top ten movies or

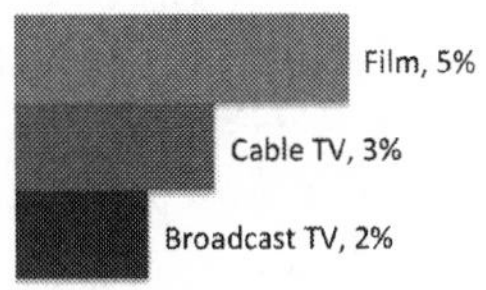


Figure 4. Latina/o shares of roles by type (2013)
*Sources*: US Population (2014 estimate): US Census, "State and County Quickfacts," http://quickfacts.census.gov/qfd/states/00000.html; "Film (Speaking)" (2013): Smith, Choueiti, and Pieper, "Race/Ethnicity in 600 Popular Films: Examining on Screen Portrayals and Behind the Camera Diversity"; "Cable TV" and "Broadcast TV" (2012–2013): Darnell Hunt and Ana-Christina Ramon, "2015 Hollywood Diversity Report: Flipping the Script" (Los Angeles: Ralph J. Bunche Center for African American Studies at UCLA, 2015).

network television shows.[29] In 2014, only 2.7 percent of lead roles in films went to Latinas/os.[30] Just two US broadcast television shows in the 2014–2015 season starred Latinas: *Jane the Virgin* and *Cristela. Cristela* was cancelled after just one season. In 2015, Gina Rodriguez became only the second Latina actor to win a lead actress Golden Globe Award when she won for *Jane the Virgin.* In her acceptance speech, Rodriguez said her win "represents a culture that wants to see themselves as heroes."[31] Even with Rodriguez's win, Latinas/os remain the lowest represented racial group compared with their percentage in the population.

### *Asian American and Pacific Islander Actors*

Asian American and Pacific Islander actors were underrepresented in film and television in 2013. They were 5.5 percent of the US population but underrepresented across the board on all screens (see fig. 5). This number improved in the 2014–2015 primetime broadcast television shows, in which Asian Americans/Pacific Islanders made up 5 percent of the series regulars.[32] But, as with African Americans, the increase in numbers was due mainly to the addition of one all-Asian show, *Fresh Off the Boat*. Despite the addition of network shows such as *Dr. Ken* and *Quantico* and streaming shows such as *Master of None* in 2015–2016, Asian Americans and Pacific Islanders were still missing from most shows. In fact, 50 percent—63 percent of all cinematic, television, or streaming stories in 2014–2015 failed to portray one speaking or named Asian or Asian American on screen.[33] When asked about the Asian "boom" in television, Ken Jeong retorted, "Three out of 409 scripted shows on television. So, is there really a boom? Maybe to white people it's a boom."[34]

The quality of Asian American and Pacific Islander roles remain low. Research shows that Asian American and Pacific Islander

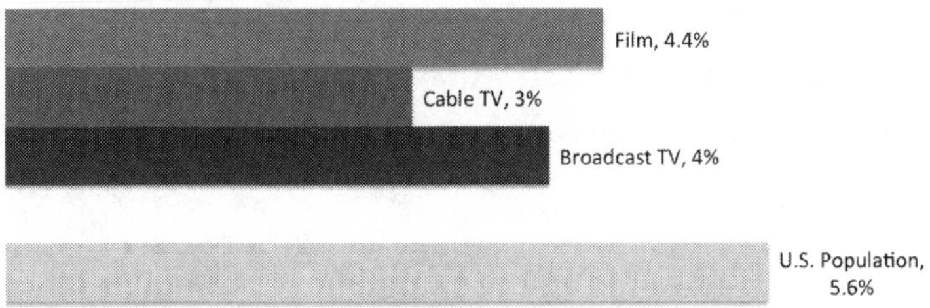


Figure 5. Asian American shares of roles by type (2013)
*Sources*: US Population (2014 estimate): US Census, "State and County Quickfacts," http://quickfacts.census.gov/qfd/states/00000.html; "Film (Speaking)" (2013): Smith, Choueiti, and Pieper, "Race/Ethnicity in 600 Popular Films: Examining on Screen Portrayals and Behind the Camera Diversity"; "Cable TV" and "Broadcast TV" (2012–2013): Darnell Hunt and Ana-Christina Ramon, "2015 Hollywood Diversity Report: Flipping the Script" (Los Angeles: Ralph J. Bunche Center for African American Studies at UCLA, 2015).

regulars on shows with multiracial casts had some of the lowest screen times and the least character complexity on primetime television.[35] Asian Americans also rarely played lead roles—only 1.3 of film leads in 2014.[36] Golden Globe–nominated Japanese American actor Masi Oka said, "It's changed in Hollywood, but only so much. . . . You can't get Asians cast in leads yet. Maybe as a second lead, but the lead is still going to be Caucasian or African American."[37] *Fresh Off the Boat* became the first network primetime show to feature an Asian American family in twenty years—an exception that proved the rule.

### *Female Actors of Color*

Female actors of color have some of the lowest numbers on screen. Women overall were underrepresented in the top one hundred films of 2013, occupying only 30 percent of speaking roles, compared with share of 50 percent in the general population.[38] Out of this low number, women of color fared the worst. The racial breakdown among female characters in the hundred top-grossing films of 2013 was as follows: 73 percent white, followed by African American (14 percent), Latina

(5 percent), and Asian (3 percent).[39] There was also a category of "otherworldly" female characters, which also came in at 3 percent—meaning that film audiences were as likely to see an alien woman as an Asian woman.[40] This underrepresentation is exacerbated by Hollywood's unwillingness to cast women of color as leads in science fiction films. Mexican/Lebanese American actor Salma Hayek recounts how she missed out on an opportunity to star in an unnamed sci-fi film when the studio would not accept her as the director's first choice: "They said to him, 'A Mexican in space?'"[41] Similarly, Scarlett Johansson plays a Japanese character, "Major Motoko Kusanagi," in fantasy film *Ghost in the Shell* (2017). Hollywood has a real discrimination problem when white aliens are more visible on the film screen than are women of color. The numbers are worse with lead roles. According to NPR television critic Eric Deggans, only three network television dramas have starred an African American woman as the main lead character since 1974.[42] Even fewer Latina and Asian American women have starred—just one each.[43]

Women of color are also less celebrated than are white women. As of 2016, Halle Berry is the only woman of color to win a best actress Oscar. As of 2016, only nine best supporting actress Oscars have gone to women of color.[44] Not until 2015 did a woman of color (Viola Davis) win an Emmy for outstanding lead actress in a dramatic series. Furthermore, women of color are consistently missing in *Vanity Fair*'s annual "young Hollywood" issue, which features popular young female actors. The few times women of color made the issue, they were relegated to the inside folds of the magazine cover, while white women graced the front.[45]

Women of color also face greater barriers as they age. Subject to an intersection of racism, sexism, and ageism, women of color over the age of forty face the fewest role options. Female actors of color over forty face fewer roles because (1) fewer projects feature people of color in romantic relationships (racism), and most roles for women are romantic partners of men (sexism); and (2) women over forty rarely get cast as romantic leads (ageism/sexism). Acclaimed African American actor Denzel Washington has never had romantic partners played by women older than thirty-five, even as he approaches sixty himself.[46] Elena, a Latina actor in her early sixties, told me about being rejected for a romantic role in her thirties:

> I once auditioned for a film, and I was ten years younger than the lead, but they still said I was too old. So, they went with someone who was—I was already in my thirties—they went with somebody who was in her twenties. The lead was in his forties. So, they want the lead to look heroic and strong, so you get . . . someone who's like a child.

Latina actor America Ferrera described the exclusion of Latina actors: "I was 18 and putting myself on tape for a movie I really wanted. I got that phone call: They cast a Latino male in another role in the film; they're not looking to cast [a Latina]."[47]

Working female actors of color over forty find that guest star and recurring roles dwindle as they age. Isabella, a Chinese American female actor in her early fifties, described to me the multiple barriers she faces as an older woman of color:

> For ethnic women, first of all, there are not a whole lot of roles you see on daytime television, on nighttime television, network or cable. . . . Seeing Asian faces and selling television are few and far between. . . . And I observe that there are less roles for women than for Asian American men. . . . There are a lot more medical shows that they would hire more older Asian American

> actors as doctors or medical people. But very seldom you'll see them hire like an older Asian American woman as medical people with lines or . . . a recurring character. Maybe walk-ons yes, but not so much like a guest star or a recurring or like even a lead in the show. I mean you can really count on two hands how many.

Hollywood deems women of color who are over the age of forty the least castable. Not only do they have fewer roles than white men and white women, but they also get cast less often than their male and younger ethnic counterparts. The racial, gender, and age biases against women of color make them the most vulnerable population among actors.

Overall, the dearth of regular and lead roles for actors of color remains a systemic problem in Hollywood. With fewer roles available, actors of color face more barriers to success. Furthermore, when actors of color do appear, they are either marginal to white leads or relegated to a few shows. Hollywood continues to block actors of color (especially women of color) from full participation. As a result, the on-screen landscape is not one of diversity and integration but one of stereotypes and segregation.

### *Earnings Gap*

Besides role barriers, actors of color also face a pay gap. The industry creates hierarchical tracks that vary by race, with white male leads making tens of millions of dollars while comparable leads of color make as little as 1 percent of that.[48] For several years running, Robert Downey Jr. (white male) has been the highest paid actor (among both males and females), at $80 million. Whites dominate the top-earning actors in Hollywood. In 2015, the ten top-earning US male actors were all white, except for two actors of color (Dwayne Johnson and

Vin Diesel),[49] while all ten top-earning female film actors were white, except for Cameron Diaz.[50] Though Cameron Diaz is part Cuban, she largely plays "white" roles that do not highlight her Latina ethnicity. Latina actor Sofia Vergara was the top-paid television actress three years in a row, earning $37 million in 2014.[51] She surpassed the top-paid television male actor, Ashton Kutcher, who earned $26 million in 2014. Even though most of her earnings come from endorsement and licensing deals and not directly from acting, Vergara demonstrates the (generally undervalued) earning potential of female actors of color. She also demonstrates the diversity gap between television and film—with television representing more people of color than do films. This is evidenced by the eighteen black television performer nominations (2015 Emmy Awards), compared with all-white film acting nominations (2015 and 2016 Academy Awards).[52]

The structural exclusion of actors of color, particularly from lead roles, makes Hollywood a discriminatory work environment. Without lead roles, actors of color are paid less well. This inability of Hollywood to conceptualize actors of color as big box-office draws and the consequent lack of inclusion and promotion perpetuate the problem. Not only does the system underrepresent and marginalize actors of color on screen, but it also keeps them away from the lucrative payouts that whites have.

## White Dominance behind the Scenes

Behind the scenes, racial discrepancies are even starker. The dominance of whites in key creative and decision-making positions (e.g., studio executives, directors, producers, writers) means more all-white casts and fewer stories featuring people of color. Even if white decision makers are not consciously racist, they can implicitly favor whites in hiring and creative decisions. As Adam Moore, national director of Equal Employment Opportunities and Diversity for the Screen Actors Guild–American Federation of Television and Radio Artists (SAG-AFTRA), told me, "There is a very persistent and rampant laziness, complacency, risk aversion that leads you back to places you found success before; that leads you back to collaborators you've had success and talent pools and story lines and all those things." Matt Damon shot down black female producer Effie Brown's desire to cast a diverse set of directors by stating, "When we're talking about diversity, you do it in the casting of the film not in the casting of the show," meaning that diversity does not apply to those working behind the scenes.[53] This type of thinking serves to justify racially homogenous Hollywood boardrooms and creative personnel (see fig. 6).

### *Media Ownership and Studio Executives*

Accepting an honorary Oscar in 2015, Spike Lee said, "It's easier to be the president of the United States as a black person than to be the head of a studio."[54] Media owners and studio executives—nearly all white males—are powerful decision makers who greenlight projects. People of color owned only 6 percent of all commercial television stations in 2013 (blacks owned 0.6 percent, Asians owned 1.4 percent, and Latinos owned 3 percent).[55] Hollywood's executive suites also severely lack people of color. In 2013, only 4 percent of television network and studio heads and 8 percent of film studio heads were people of color. Compared with the rest of corporate America, Hollywood executives rank last in terms of racial diversity. In a 2010 study of Fortune 500 companies, only one in twenty executive managers in the media and entertainment business were people of color, compared with one in ten executive managers over all business sectors.[56] The first Asian American studio executive—Kevin Tsujihara, CEO of Warner Bros.—was appointed as recently as 2013.[57]

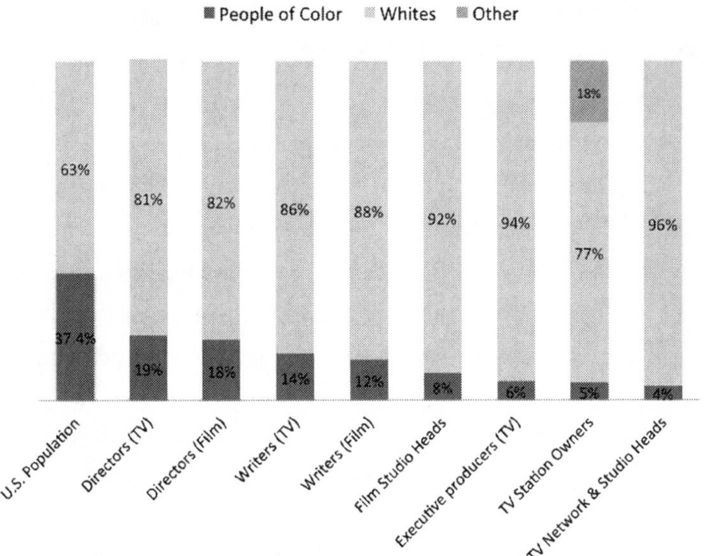


Figure 6. Hollywood behind-the-scenes personnel of color
*Sources*: US Population (2014 estimate): US Census, "State and County Quickfacts," http://quickfacts.census.gov/qfd/states/00000.html; "Directors (TV)" (2014–2015): Directors Guild of America, "DGA TV Diversity Report: Employer Hiring of Women Directors Shows Modest Improvement; Women and Minorities Continue to Be Excluded in First-Time Hiring" (Los Angeles: Directors Guild of America, 2015); "Directors (Film)," "Film Studio Heads," and "TV Network & Studio Heads" (2013): Hunt and Ramon, "2015 Hollywood Diversity Report: Flipping the Script;" "Executive Producers (TV)" and "Writers (TV)" (2013–2014): Darnell Hunt, "WGAW 2015 TV Staffing Brief" (Los Angeles: Writers Guild of America, West, 2015); "TV Station Owner" (2013): Federal Communications Commission, "Report on Ownership of Commercial Broadcast Stations" (Washington, DC: Federal Communications Commission, 2014).

Adding more executives of color and female executives can broaden the diversity of actors in film and television. Zola Mashariki—one of the few African American studio executives in Hollywood—was instrumental in releasing *12 Years a Slave*, featuring an international black cast and crew and winning multiple Oscars, including best picture and best supporting actress, Lupita Nyong'o.[58] Mashariki describes her desire to make films featuring African Americans: "When I came to Hollywood, I wanted to make many different kinds of films, but I think I would have died if I didn't have [the] opportunity to tell stories about people who looked like me."[59] African American female actor Sonia Sohn describes how her character on Home Box Office's (HBO) *The Wire* was supposed to get killed in the first season, but was saved by a white female HBO executive who wanted to preserve the diversity of a black lesbian character.[60] Given that media owners and studio executives have the power to green-light a project (that is, financially approve it to move from development to production), Hollywood needs a more diverse boardroom to support and promote projects featuring people of color.

### *Directors*

Whites make up the majority of directors. In 2013, film directors were 82.2 percent white. Whites directed 82 percent of all episodes in the 2014–2015 network and cable television season. The racial groups represented by directors of color in the 2013–2014 season were 7 percent African American, 3 percent Latino, and 2 percent Asian American.[61] In the same season, 84 percent of first-time television directors were white, demonstrating that directors of color have a much harder time getting a foot in the door than do their white counterparts.[62] When examining the intersection of race and gender, white men are overrepresented as directors. White men are only 37 percent of the US population,[63] yet they represented nearly double and triple that percentage as television and film directors, respectively. Specifically, they directed 69 percent of all episodes in the 2014–2015 network and cable television season. White men also directed 90 percent of the 2014 summer movies.[64] In contrast, white women directed 13 percent of the 2014–2015 season television episodes, men of color directed 15 percent, and women of color directed only 3 percent.[65] Women of color were consistently the least represented group among directors. Out of seven hundred films in 2014, women of color directed only four (less than 1 percent).[66]

Hollywood's failure to recognize directors of color further compounds the problem. All of the Academy Awards best picture films had white directors until 2014, when *12 Years a Slave*—directed by black British director Steve McQueen—won best picture. In eighty-seven years of the Academy Awards, only five best director Oscars went to directors of color (all men): two to Ang Lee (for *Brokeback Mountain* in 2006 and for *Life of Pi* in 2013), one to Alfonso Cuarón (for *Gravity* in 2014), and two to Alejandro González Iñárritu (for *Birdman* in 2015 and for *The Revenant* in 2016). No woman of color has ever been nominated for a best director Academy Award. Furthermore, with the exception of *Life of Pi,* all of the films that won best director Oscars had white-centered storylines. This perpetuates a culture of validating whiteness in Hollywood films.

To remedy this problem, Hollywood can begin by employing more directors of color. Hiring directors of color can increase the overall quantity and quality of people of color represented in film and television. Directors of color are key to increasing the number of people of color represented on screen. Studies of the top-grossing films in 2008 and 2010 found that films with black directors had more than six times the number of black characters, compared with films with non-black directors.[67] In contrast, white film and television directors, such as Woody Allen and Lena Dunham, have had no problem erasing people of color from stories set in diverse settings such as New York City.[68]

Many directors of color feature more complex portraits of people of color in their projects than do white directors. African American female director Ava DuVernay describes how she brought her intersectional racial and gender perspective when developing her film *Selma* (2014):

> I wasn't interested in making a white-savior movie; I was interested in making a movie centered on the people of Selma. You have to bring in some context for what it was like to live in the racial terrorism that was going on in the deep south at that time. The four little girls have to be there, and then you have to bring in the women. So I started adding women.[69]

As an African American female director, DuVernay brings her vision and perspective to highlight black characters, especially black women. Similarly, Latino director Robert Rodriguez discusses his motivation to bring Latinas/os into the mainstream in his movie *Spy Kids:*

> It's nice seeing really cool, heroic characters who are named the Cortez family . . . and it's great being able to do that in a very mainstream film. And I hope that one of the audience's reactions is that there will be kids going around wanting to be Carmen Cortez. And I like being able to do that without being overly preachy about it. Rather than doing it as a niche film, for a niche Latino market, instead I want it to play to everybody. And have them identify with the characters.[70]

This intention to feature Latina/o heroes in family-friendly films is something directors of color such as Robert Rodriguez uniquely bring to the screen. Directors of color often have a personal motivation to represent people of color in complex ways—not as racial caricatures or token sidekicks.

In contrast, white directors often racially stereotype and artistically stunt actors of color. Ed, an African American actor in his late sixties, tells me how white directors

> see all black people the same. They see us like they saw us, or they thought they saw us, in the forties or fifties, you know? So when

you get a part, they immediately want you to be broad and they want you to use all the slang and they want you to curse, and a lot these things isn't necessary. But this is how they see us. That prevents a lot of good performances.

Our media world will be richer if directors come from diverse backgrounds. Directors of color are more likely than white directors to make racially diverse films. Directors of color are also more intentional than white directors about quality representation of all racial groups. In particular, investing in first-time directors of color will help them succeed—especially because directors of color are "more likely to continue on in television directing than the rest of the pool," according to Directors Guild of America president Paris Barclay.[71] By targeting first-time directors of color, Hollywood can develop directors of color earlier in their careers, leading to greater chances of success and longevity. Hiring directors of color is a necessary but insufficient step toward eradicating the racist tropes embedded in Hollywood storytelling. Directors (of all racial backgrounds) must also be intentional in creating complex and counter-stereotypical representations of people of color.

### *Executive Producers and Writers*

Whites make up 92 percent of all television executive producers, also called showrunners. Television executive producers are the creative backbone of television shows. According to the Writers Guild of America (WGA), the executive producer is "in charge of pre-production, production, and post-production. In other words, everything."[72] Specifically, television executive producers hire and manage writing staffs and oversee scripts, all of which involve deciding which types of stories and characters will appear in the final production. Executive producers are not only the creative and casting decision makers for television shows but are key to whether the shows get made at all. The best predictor of whether a television pilot gets selected by networks is whether it has an established executive producer of a prior successful series.[73]

Television writing jobs have traditionally served as the track for becoming an executive producer. Because whites make up the majority of writers in Hollywood, they dominate the pipeline. Whites account for 86.3 percent of television writers and 88.2 percent of film writers. White (male) showrunners and writers receive preferential treatment from television network executives. For example, HBO entrusted two white male novelists who had never run a television show with its biggest project, *Game of Thrones*. One journalist pointed out that although they rose to the challenge, "it's hugely unlikely they would have gotten a similar chance had they not been white men."[74] Network executives also pressure showrunners to maintain an all-white writer's room. Glen Mazzara, a white male executive producer on *The Shield* and *The Walking Dead*, discussed receiving pushback from network executives when trying to bring in more writers of color. A network executive asked him whether he had an "Asian fetish" because he had "two Asians on a writing staff."[75] Resistance can also come from white writers, who may perceive writers of color as token diversity hires and treat them with disrespect and disdain.[76]

When writers' rooms are filled with white writers, storylines tend to revolve around white characters. Leslie, a white female actor and casting director in her forties, explains to me, "As long as middle-aged white America is writing roles, middle-aged white men will get the better roles, and the rest of us pick up what's left." Kinchi, a Japanese American male actor in his forties, tells me about the bias he sees among white male writers: "They write what they see in their head. White guy writes a role about a guy and his girlfriend; he doesn't see an Asian guy in that role. He just doesn't." The dominance of white male writers also result in more stereotyped characters of color. Del, a black female actor and casting director in her forties, describes how white male writers tend to create more limited and stereotyped characters:

> The people that are writing the scripts . . . usually white people, usually white boys, and they're coming from a very limited world. So, they're going to put you in a certain role. I mean that, and they're the ones in power, they're the ones that are making the decisions. So, of course, stereotyping's going to happen, and that's going to continue to happen until somebody does something different to make a change.

Consequently, the fictional worlds created by film and television writers reflect the racial imbalance within this sector.

Showrunners of color, in contrast, are more likely to create diverse shows. Shonda Rhimes, an African American female executive producer at ABC, casts actors of color in all of her shows (*Grey's Anatomy, Private Practice, Scandal,* and *How to Get Away with Murder*). Two of her shows have black women leads, both of which made history—*Scandal* with Kerry Washington as the first drama to feature a black woman in nearly forty years, and *How to Get Away with Murder* with Viola Davis as the first woman of color to ever win an "outstanding lead actress in a dramatic series" Emmy. Lee Daniels, an African American male film director and television executive producer, created *Empire* (Fox), which features a predominantly African American cast and writing staff. One of the African American writers, Josh Allen, describes what Lee Daniels brings to *Empire:* "I think the authenticity above all is important. There should be somebody in the room that's like, 'That sounds like some white people stuff,' 'cause you hear that from communities of color.

So having that come from the top down really infuses how we tell those stories."[77] Nahnatchka Khan, an Iranian American female television showrunner, produces *Fresh Off the Boat* (ABC), a sitcom about a Taiwanese American family and the first Asian American show to air beyond a single season on broadcast television. Khan's writing staff includes many writers of color—nearly half are of East Asian or South Asian descent.[78] Indian American actor, comedian, and showrunner Aziz Ansari describes the motivation to cast an Asian American actor in *Master of None:* "When we were looking for an Asian actor . . . my fellow creator, Alan Yang, asked me: 'How many times have you seen an Asian guy kiss someone in TV or film?' After a long hard think, we came up with two (Steven Yeun on 'The Walking Dead' and Daniel Dae Kim on 'Lost'). It made me realize how important it was not to give up on our search."[79]

More executive producers and writers of color behind the camera—especially those who do not subscribe to the old race ideology that has fueled the stereotyped portrayals of people of color—translate into more stories featuring actors of color. Incidentally, all of the aforementioned shows have high ratings, particularly among audiences of color. In fact, *Empire* was the breakout broadcast television show of 2015, with increased ratings week after week, ending with a season high of nearly 17 million total viewers.[80] Consequently, shows featuring people of color are not just good for society but good for business.

### *Talent Agents and Casting Directors*

Talent agents and casting directors are gatekeepers that guard the status quo. Though they do not have the final decision on casting, they serve a filtering purpose. Most working actors have to go through their talent agents and casting directors before seeing a producer or director. Talent agents choose actors to represent as clients and pick which actor clients to send out to auditions, including sending in headshots (actors' photos and résumés). Casting directors provide casting information to Breakdown Services (the leading distributor of casting notices) based on their readings of scripts, screen actors to bring in for auditions, and select actors to recommend to producers and directors. If talent agents and casting directors harbor societal and industry biases, they can perpetuate the institutional exclusion and stereotyping of actors of color.

TALENT AGENTS. Talent agents create opportunities, procure and negotiate employment for clients, and counsel them in the development of their careers. Working actors are not legally allowed to negotiate contracts or book jobs on their own, and they rely on talent agents as intermediaries, who typically take a 10 percent commission from the work they procure for actors. Actors can have one theatrical agent (who covers film, television, and theater), along with a commercial agent who helps them book commercial advertisements. Agents range in influence, with some just submitting headshots and others acting as gatekeepers to the top studios. The elite talent agencies, such as Creative Artists Agency (CAA), William Morris Endeavor (WME), and United Talent Agency (UTA), ensure their clients exclusive access to Hollywood projects denied to the average actor. These top talent agencies have the power to package entire projects—including a script, a producer, a director, and actor(s)—thereby giving them creative and administrative sway in the industry.[81] Consequently, talent agents are not only the first line of gatekeepers responsible for submitting actors but can play a major role in assembling and producing projects.

Talent agents can keep actors of color from equal access to jobs—both by underrepresenting clients of color and by limiting their clients of color to stereotyped roles. Some talent agents intentionally exclude or limit their number of clients of color compared with their white clients. Chinese American actor Lucy Liu's first agents took her only on a freelance basis because they had no Asian American clients.[82] Freddie, an African American male actor in his mid-forties, told me how an agent refused to represent him because they already had "two people just like you" (that is, African Americans) despite having forty-six clients who were "all white." When actors of color are denied access or are not prioritized by talent agents, their job prospects are limited. The barriers get worse as the talent agencies grow in prestige. The top agencies (CAA, WME, and UTA) are the worst offenders in underrepresenting clients of color.[83] In 2013, lead actors of color on broadcast television shows were underrepresented by a factor of nearly seven-to-one at the top talent agencies.[84] The top agencies also failed to represent people of color behind the scenes. Of all broadcast television show creators represented at the top agencies, just 4.2 percent were people of color; of cable television show creators represented, 9.1 percent were people of color; of film directors represented, 15.9 percent were directors of color; and of film writers represented, 11.2 percent were writers of color.[85] Because top agencies are the conduits to major career-building projects, lack of access to them puts actors and other artists of color at a severe disadvantage.

Talent agents may attribute their racial exclusions to supply and demand. One African American female talent agent told me that because there are fewer roles for actors of color, agencies "wouldn't want to bring somebody on who's going to compete with their top bookers" because "the industry's so limited." This rationale precludes the possibility that talent agents can send actors of color to audition for all roles, regardless of race and gender. In fact, some actors of color in my study had asked their agents to submit them for white roles and had successfully landed them. However, many actors of color said their talent agents limited their ability to audition for roles outside their racial and ethnic categories. Meera, an Indian American actor in her twenties, told me how she has to fight her commercial agent (often unsuccessfully) to stop sending her on Indian-specific auditions, which she says she never books. Jessica, a Hapa (of mixed racial heritage, with partial roots in Asian and/or Pacific Islander ancestry) actor, told me how even though she often gets mistaken for Latina in her everyday life, her talent agent refuses to send her for roles outside her ethnicity: "She does not send me out for Latin roles. And I have had this conversation with her time and again. And I said, 'Look, you are promoting me as Eurasian,' which is what I am. 'But I'm Filipino, which means I have Spanish blood in me, which means if I could speak Spanish, you should be sending me out.' She's not comfortable sending me out on that." Some talent agents pigeonhole actors of color (even multiracial actors of color) into specific, immutable racial categories, and are unwilling to conceptualize them in nontraditional roles. In turn, this limits the audition pool to white actors. Even worse, some talent agents send their white clients to audition for characters of color. One white female actor told me she had pushed her commercial agent to send her out for "Latin stuff" and then successfully "booked the part of Maria Conchita." She admitted that she even signed in with a fake Spanish surname at casting calls. Hollywood creates a double standard by funneling actors of color into race-specific roles while casting white actors in every role regardless of race.

Talent agents further constrain actors of color by submitting them to stereotyped roles. According to the founder of Breakdown Services, even if a casting breakdown does not specify race or gender, agents typically submit actors based on racial and gender stereotypes—such as submitting only women for nurse roles.[86] Taija, an African American actor in her late thirties, describes how an agent put her "in a box" based on the "color of [her] skin." She further elaborates on this experience: "I had a meeting with an agent. I haven't been in the office more than a minute, and he just starts pegging me for the tough street type. And I'm sitting there like just in awe because I haven't said a word, and he's never seen me act. He didn't know that I had actually played leading lady roles. And it was very insulting because it was almost that feeling of being stereotyped." Talent agents reinforce a biased system by siphoning actors of color into racially stereotyped roles. One Latina actor said, "I've only gotten roles playing a nanny or housekeeper. There is prejudice, but then even your agent is responsible for that."[87]

CASTING DIRECTORS. Casting directors are hired by studios, networks, and production companies to present actors for consideration by gathering groups of actors who would be good for each role. Though they are not responsible for creating roles or even final casting decisions, they are crucial gatekeepers. According to one casting director, "It's a curious job. You're in a position of influence but not power: we don't ultimately decide who gets the job, but we can influence who's in the frame."[88] Based on headshots, recommendations, and personal knowledge (of actors from previous auditions or social networks), casting directors choose which actors to audition and then, based on their auditions, which actors to recommend.

Casting directors can play a big role in reproducing racism in the Hollywood industry. In the early days of Hollywood, before the formation of the Screen Actors Guild in 1933, African American actors were at the mercy of casting directors, who dictated all of their roles and negotiated their contracts because most talent agencies refused to represent African American actors.[89] Today, casting directors—at the behest of film and television directors—can remain an obstruction to actors of color, as described by Asian American actor Pun Bandhu: "Managers and agents tried to get us in those doors, but they were never able to get us auditions, because the casting directors are only filling the directives of directors. Unless they are told they are looking for multicultural, the default is Caucasian, and that's disturbing."[90]

Casting directors can also harbor racial bias, which further limits actors of color. One casting director told me about a common racial bias among casting directors:

> I work with a lot of different people, and Asians are a challenge to cast because most casting directors feel as though they're not very expressive. They're very shut down in their emotions. . . . If it's a look thing for business, where they come in and they're at a computer, or if they're like a scientist or something like that, they'll do that; but if it's something where they really have to act and to get some kind of performance out of, it's a challenge.

By conflating all Asian American actors into a single "not very expressive" group, casting directors effectively ignore the diversity of personalities, histories, languages, and cultures among Asian Americans. This stereotype of Asians lacking expression and emotions is derivative of the stoic and passive Charlie Chan character popularized by Hollywood film and television.

Casting directors also display their racial bias when they cannot distinguish between stereotype and truth during auditions. One of the first roles Indian American actor Aasif Mandvi auditioned for was a "snake charmer." The casting director asked whether he could "actually snake charm." Desperate to land the role, Mandvi told the casting director, "Well I *am* Indian so it's probably in my DNA." But in the end, Mandvi said, they cast "a white guy."[91] Casting directors also tell actors of color to act "more" black, Asian, or Latin, often based on racial stereotypes. Because such statements can be ambiguous, actors of color are left to guess at what stereotypes to invoke.

Michael, an African American actor in his forties, told me about his confusion when asked by a casting director to "be a little more black." When asked to clarify, the director asked, "Can you be more jive, you know what I mean?" Michael said he tried to do "every best stereotype" he could think of, but did not get the job. They ended up casting a "white guy in the role." The idea that there is a way to "be more black" reduces entire populations to a narrow set of racial stereotypes. As an African American actor, Michael cannot be any "more black" than he already is. Furthermore, in both of the examples, the casting directors ultimately cast white actors, which shows that their directives to perform racial stereotypes applied only to actors of color, not the role itself.

Casting directors also pass over African American actors for roles based on their skin color. For some, being too fair-skinned is a reason for exclusion. Dawn, a light-skinned African American actor in her thirties, describes her horror at being told by a casting director that she was too light to play black characters in commercials:

> I've had a casting director say that I—this is horrible—that I'm so light that for commercials, I barely pass the paper bag test[92] . . . because when they see you on that commercial, you might be there for three seconds, but they want to know automatically what you are. Are you black? Are you white? What are you? And so he said that I might come off as not being black. So I probably won't book a lot of commercials.

At the same time, many light-skinned African American actors enjoy greater access to film and television, while darker-skinned African American actors—particularly women—often find themselves excluded or stereotyped as less attractive.[93] For example, the *Straight Outta Compton* casting call listed "fine" girls who "should be light-skinned," and girls who are "not in good shape" with "medium to dark skin tone."[94] This intersection of colorism and sexism places additional constraints on female actors of color.

There is a racial disparity in how casting directors interact with actors. Out of the thirty white actors I interviewed, none was ever told to be "more white" or judged based on his or her skin color. Currently, nothing protects actors of color from these discriminatory actions based on their race. Overtly discriminatory determinants based on skin color and statements such as "Be more Asian" or "Be more black" would not pass in any other work setting. More than just creative notes on an actor's performance, such racially stereotyped requests constitute racial harassment, a form of employment discrimination that violates Title VII of the Civil Rights Act of 1964. The government can monitor these practices more closely and protect actors of color from being ostracized if they choose to come forth and report racial harassment.

Gatekeepers such as talent agents and casting directors can have an enormous impact on the casting and stereotyping of actors of color. Studio heads, directors, and producers do not even get the opportunity to hire actors of color if these actors cannot make it past talent agents and casting directors due to racial bias. Consequently, more intervention at this gatekeeping level can help diversify Hollywood. Casting directors can help, not hinder, more diverse casting. Casting director Jennifer Euston, who won the 2014 Emmy for casting *Orange Is the New Black*, is a leader in diverse casting. Even when Euston is handed scripts that almost exclusively feature white men, she says, "You do your best to sort of offer alternatives, if you can."[95] Like Euston, all talent agents and casting directors can be more mindful of offering actors of color for complex roles (typically reserved for white men) rather than clichéd stereotypes.

What W.E.B. Du Bois said in 1903 still holds true today: "The problem of the Twentieth Century is the problem of the color-line."[96]

The overvisibility of whites and undervisibility of people of color in film and television buttress the racial hierarchy. The dominance of white men across all Hollywood ranks gives them the power to control and disseminate ideas and images that reflect their lived experiences. As James Lull states:

> Owners and managers of media industries can produce and reproduce the content, inflections, and tones of ideas favorable to them far more easily than other social groups because they manage key socializing institutions, thereby guaranteeing that their points of view are constantly and attractively cast into the public arena.[97]

A majority white male workforce behind the scenes contributes to the hiring of white actors above and beyond their representation in US demographics. In any other industry, this would violate Title VII of the Civil Rights Act, which "prohibits employment discrimination based on race, color, religion, sex and national origin."[98] By hiding behind the First Amendment, Hollywood justifies discriminatory hiring practices and perpetuates a white world.

# 2

# HOLLYWOOD'S COLORBLIND RACISM

*I'm not interested in diversity, I'm interested in brilliance.*

—Nick Stevens

Nick Stevens is a top Hollywood talent agent who has worked at United Talent Agency (UTA) and William Morris Endeavor (WME). A white man in his fifties, Stevens has an impressive client list that includes A-list white actors Ben Stiller, Jack Black, Owen Wilson, Seth Rogen, Jonah Hill, and Amy Poehler, as well as writer-producer Judd Apatow.[1] Ben Stiller made this statement about Stevens: "I think Nick Stevens is a unique entity in this business: an agent with integrity, a point of view, and, most of all, humanity."[2] When I asked Stevens about the lack of racial and gender diversity in Hollywood, he readily acknowledged that Hollywood "sucks at" diversity, but quickly added that he is "not interested in diversity, but brilliance."[3] This statement epitomizes Hollywood's ambivalence about diversity. On the one hand, Hollywood purports to be an industry made up of progressive, open-minded artists who publicly condemn racism and support diversity. On the other hand, it is one of the most powerful and flagrant (even if unconscious) perpetuators of racism through exclusionary and stereotyped storytelling and casting practices. At the root of this reasoning is a flawed meritocracy: if actors are "brilliant" enough, their race should not factor into their chances at success. The idea that intentionally casting actors of color will somehow dilute the "brilliance" of the talent pool effectively ensures their exclusion. Hollywood refuses to acknowledge that it is not an equal playing field, and brilliance is not measured in a vacuum. This is the case with the Academy Awards, given to the supposedly most brilliant actors of our times, who happen to be mostly white and chosen by a majority white male membership. In response to accusations of racism in failing to nominate a single actor of color, one anonymous Academy member said, "I'm very offended by the idea that some people are calling us racists—race was the furthest thing from my mind when I cast my ballot."[4] The inability of the Hollywood elite to recognize or acknowledge their own racial biases perpetuates the problem.

Hollywood maintains the racial status quo through colorblind racism, or the attribution of white dominance to individual merit and cultural explanations, while denying institutional discrimination.[5] White director Steven Spielberg, in critiquing the Academy's decision to strip non-active members of their voting rights, says this: "I don't believe that there is inherent or dormant racism because of the amount of white Academy members. . . . Look, I have two black children, you know? I've been colorblind my entire life."[6] The media, according to cultural theorist Stuart Hall, reproduces dominant ideologies under an air of neutrality.[7] It is this air of colorblind neutrality that allows Hollywood to continue its practice of excluding people of color without sanction. Colorblind racism allows white decision makers and creative personnel to divest themselves of any social or moral responsibility while maintaining hegemonic control of the industry. Colorblind racism also exists in the larger US society, where more than 80 percent of white Americans deny the role of race in job, income, and housing discrepancies between whites and blacks.[8] Hollywood began employing colorblind rhetoric after the Equal Employment Opportunity Commission (EEOC) tried to prosecute the industry for racial discrimination.[9] Hollywood rebranded itself as an "open door" industry to all races and attributed any racial difference to fair competition.[10] In addition, it curtailed any government or civil rights demand for affirmative action by labeling it "preferential treatment" and "reverse racism." This is still the case today. Although Hollywood industry personnel affirm the existence of racial inequality, they deflect blame onto colorblind factors. Three of the most common forms of blame are (1) blame the talent (that is, Hollywood blames actors of color for lacking the numbers and skills); (2) blame what you know (that is, white Hollywood writers naturalize racial bias based on their life experiences); and (3) blame the market (that is, Hollywood naturalizes racial bias by deflecting it onto imagined audience preferences, which drive market dynamics).

## Blame the Talent

Hollywood sees casting as purely merit based and blames actors of color for not being up to par. The assumption of an equal playing field is a key component of colorblind racism. The idea that everyone has an equal opportunity to "make it" means that people who do not succeed must not be "good enough." However, a study of casting notices reveals that the problem is not a lack of talent but a lack of roles written for actors of color.[11] White actors have access to the majority of the written roles in Hollywood (77 percent of casting notices), shutting other groups of color out from consideration.[12] As a result, actors of color have fewer work opportunities, irrespective of their skill sets. Viola Davis said this about the lack of roles in Hollywood: "The only thing that separates women of color from anyone else is opportunity. You cannot win an Emmy for roles that are simply not there."[13] The systematic exclusion of actors of color creates a vicious cycle in which actors of color have less access to on-the-job skills, professional recognition, and social networks. Because of systemic exclusion, actors and other artists of color have less experience, which then bars them from consideration. HBO's president of programming, Michael Lombardo, describes this problem:

> People say, "I want the most experienced person." And the minute you say that, you're cutting out, by and large, women, people of color, and you're left with white dudes. And, nothing wrong with white dudes—I'm one of them—but there has to be a decision made that the experience on a résumé is not the sine qua non for success as an executive. And everyone's on the same page that it's the right thing. I think unfortunately everyone wants somebody else to take a gamble on someone whose résumé doesn't reflect the kind of experience they need.[14]

Another common "blame the talent" excuse is the complaint that there are not enough actors of color. One African American female talent agent told me that among agents there is a perceived shortage of Asian American actors. When I asked whether she had contacted East West Players (the leading Asian American theater group in the nation, located in Los Angeles), she said she had never heard of it. An unwillingness to go outside traditional venues to find actors of color is a common problem among Hollywood personnel. As Adam Moore, the national director of equal employment opportunity (EEO) and diversity for the Screen Actors Guild–American Federation of Television and Radio Artists (SAG-AFTRA), explains:

> People just get frustrated. "No I can't find them, they're not out there, so I'm just not going to look anymore." As opposed to you might have to go to places that you don't normally go. Maybe the ten agents you normally work with or have for the last ten years, maybe their rosters aren't as diverse as you want, but it doesn't mean there aren't people out there representing them who are qualified for the work. They probably just aren't in the places you're used to looking.

Because white gatekeepers have mainly white social networks, their knowledge of actors of color is limited. One Latina actor told me, "I have a good friend of mine who was a [white] producer, a really well-known producer of sitcoms. And he once called me to ask something about a casting choice because the only Latinos he knew were his gardener and maid. He doesn't—he just doesn't—socialize. . . . So, they wanted to put Latinos in, but they only knew the maids and the gardeners." Instead of acknowledging their own ignorance or taking responsibility for not investing in a deep and thorough search, Hollywood gatekeepers would rather blame a lack of qualified talent.

Hollywood also blames the exclusion of actors of color on a lack of skill and excellence. In 1999, Fox Entertainment President Doug Herzog downplayed the fact that none of the Fox prime-time television series featured a single person of color by saying he wanted "the best show on the air."[15] Similarly, when asked why no black characters appear in his films (many of which are set in ethnically diverse New York City), Oscar-winning director Woody Allen said, "You don't hire people based on race. You hire people based on who is correct for the part. The implication is that I'm deliberately not hiring black actors, which is stupid. I cast only what's right for the part. Race, friendship means nothing to me except who is right for the part."[16] Allen denied any personal racism by claiming he hires the person who is "right for the part." Given that whites are more likely to hire other whites, who is "best" and "right" is likely to skew white. One of the very few black actors cast in Allen's films is Hazelle Goodman, who played a prostitute in *Deconstructing Harry* (1997).[17] This tendency to limit actors of color to stereotyped roles prevents them from consideration for many lead roles. African American actor Gabrielle Union dismisses the "blame the talent" excuse: "So when you're saying, 'We just went with the best person,' that's all good and well if every person was considered. But every person isn't considered, so this idea of the best person is sort of a random, made-up thing to make up for a lack of inclusion in the audition process."[18] When white gatekeepers are reticent when it comes to exerting an additional effort to recruit actors of color, they end up relying on the larger pool of white actors. The "best" person is really the most convenient.

Hollywood also blames the talent by pointing to the few successful actors of color as evidence of meritocracy. In my interviews, a white male actor and acting teacher pointed to celebrities of color, such as Forrest Whittaker and Oprah, as evidence that hard work and focus are sufficient for overcoming any obstacles in the industry. However, the presence of a few token celebrities of color does not prove racial equity. In fact, Samuel L. Jackson says the film industry often seems to have tunnel vision when it comes to black talent: "There is an A-list . . . and if they can't get us, they say, 'Well, we'll wait till we can.' They're not looking for the next us."[19] Using the few stars of color to blame actors of color for not working hard enough assumes falsely that Hollywood is an equal playing field where everyone has the same opportunities for success.

Blaming the talent is such an endemic rationale that even some people of color espouse it. Kenan Thompson, an African American cast member of *Saturday Night Live* (*SNL*, NBC), blames the lack of black women on SNL on not being able to "find ones that are ready."[20] Similarly, an Asian American male writer-director blames the lack of trained Asian American actors on the Asian American culture, in which Asian parents dissuade their children from entering the entertainment industry. Though there may be some truth in these observations, they focus on outcomes rather than root causes. They fail to account for structural barriers that prevent actors of color from gaining adequate professional experience to be "ready." Furthermore, the dearth of successful actors of color makes the occupational field less attractive to communities of color, particularly immigrants. When there are so few successful actors of color, the risk may seem too high for some groups of color. Consequently, the root cause is structural, not individual.

Sometimes Hollywood blames an entire racial group for their low numbers in Hollywood. Specifically, casting directors blame Asian American actors for being unexpressive and therefore less castable. This generalization pigeonholes Asians into very narrow stereotypes, while excluding them from the majority of roles—particularly leads. Mako, a veteran Oscar-nominated Japanese American actor, describes the systematic exclusion of Asian Americans: "Asian-American actors have never been treated as full-time actors. We're always hired as part-timers. That is, producers call us when they need us for only race-specific roles. If a part was seen as too 'demanding,' that part often went to a non-Asian."[21] This prejudice against Asian American actors denies them employment and skill-building opportunities central to career advancement. Thomas, a Chinese American male actor in his mid-thirties, describes to me the structural racism that prevents Asian American actors from improving their skills: "It's not a lack of talent. I think it's a lack of opportunity to really spread your wings and get really strong. . . . It's very hard to get better when you have a one- or two-liner here and there. . . . It's like how can you become a great marathon runner if you're only allowed to sprint twenty-five yards?" Hollywood would rather blame actors of color for lacking numbers and skills than admit a systemic bias that prevents them from gaining the necessary exposure to showcase their talent. As one African American female actor told me, "Nobody can tell you're a good actor with eight lines."

Hollywood also claims "reverse racism" to deny the existence of structural inequality. In 1972, African American activists and artists formed the Coalition Against Blaxploitation to protest "the power exploitation of the black condition in America by the white-owned, white-controlled, and white-financed motion picture industry."[22] In response, the Motion Picture Association of America (MPAA)—a trade association that represents the major Hollywood studios—dismissed the coalition's claims of discrimination and framed the lack of African Americans in the industry as a natural outcome of competition between groups.[23] Instead of acknowledging institutional bias, the MPAA accused the group of "reverse discrimination" and asking for "a handout."[24] The usage of accusations of reverse racism to prevent structural changes to Hollywood's racist system continues to this day. In 2015, a *Deadline Hollywood* article critiqued the trend of "ethnic" castings in the 2015 television season as reverse racism. The author wrote, "Some agents have signaled that, instead of opening the field for actors of any race to compete for any role in a color-blind manner, there has [*sic*] been a significant number of parts designated as ethnic this year, making them off-limits for Caucasian actors."[25] Reverse racism dismisses the historical exclusion of people of color and frames white domination as evidence of white superiority. Any increase in the number of people of color within film and television is therefore attributed to quotas rather than talent. This type of thinking is not only flawed, but also a major barrier to racial progress. As one critic said, "If one group maintains an apartheid chokehold on the arts even as the country grows more diverse, there's a problem with the pipeline, not the talent pool."[26]

## Blame "What You Know"

Hollywood writers use the "Write what you know" mantra as a defense against accusations of racism. This rationale, at its core, naturalizes racial segregation: whites simply prefer to be with other whites. Therefore, whites cannot be blamed if all they have are white relationships and experiences on which to base their writing. By reducing the creative process to personal experience, white writers divert attention away from their racial bias.[27] When asked about the lack of blacks in his ABC network show *Wasteland* (1999), set in New York City, white male show-creator Kevin Williamson stated that New York looks that way because that is his "experience of it."[28] Given that New York City has a population consisting of 25.5 percent blacks, 28.6 percent Latinos, and 12.7 percent Asian Americans,[29] writers are intentionally eliminating 66.8 percent of the population. Similarly, Lena Dunham, in response to criticism about the lack of actors of color on her hit HBO show *Girls* (also set in New York City), said she writes "super-specific" to her "experience" as a "half-Jew, half-WASP," rather than experiences of women of color she "can't speak to accurately."[30] To fend off critiques of racism when writing for all-white casts set in diverse locations, white writers personalize the writing process to their life experiences.

The "Write what you know" rationale is pervasive throughout Hollywood, even among actors of color. Latina actor Sofia Vergara exonerates writers thus: "I cannot blame the writers because when you're a writer, you write about what you know. So you cannot tell an American writer to just write about some other culture and think it will be as natural as writing about an American person."[31] Similarly, Cassie, a forty-five-year-old African American female actor, attributes the overrepresentation of white roles not to racism but to white writers' lack of exposure to blacks: "Well, the white actors get more [roles] because there's white writers writing it. See, you can't say they're prejudiced or nothing because they're white—white to white people. They're white, that's what they know. . . . I mean, how many producers know black people, really? They don't hang out on Crenshaw." Cassie takes the prejudice factor out and attributes the lack of black roles to a lack of social contact between white writers and African Americans. Similarly, Isabel, a Chinese American actor in her late forties, ascribes stereotyping to writing outside one's race: "I think until the script or the writer who created an Asian character knows the culture, they will always be writing from the outside. . . . So, nine out of ten times when you get a script with an Asian character, the lines are usually not quite how an Asian or an Asian American would speak. . . . But they write it in broken English.'" Too often, the "Write what you know" rationale lets white writers off the hook for their racial bias or lack of racial awareness.

Despite its wide acceptance, the "Write what you know" rationale is fundamentally flawed. First, the idea that white writers can never write authentic stories about people of color is problematic. It falsely assumes that people of color are defined only by their race and glosses over national, ethnic, and geographic diversity within racial groups. This rationale also gives primacy to race, avoiding the ways gender, sexuality, class, age, and other factors also influence experiences. Furthermore, it assumes immutable differences between racial groups—marginalizing people of color as racial "others." This is false because white writers never mention racial kinship when they create white characters. In an interview, writer-director Christopher Nolan describes how he based the (white male) protagonist of *Interstellar* (2014) on his own "underlying moral quandaries, the underlying emotional stakes," and "fatherhood."[32] These are common human qualities that are not restricted to a single race. Nonetheless, many white writers see emotional depth and relational experiences as exclusive to white characters.

The "Write what you know" rationale also fails to account for creativity and imagination in the writing process. White male screenwriter and director Scott Cooper describes his multipronged writing process: "I tend to write from personal experience, from research, and from imagination."[33] Cooper set his film *Out of the Furnace* (2013) in Braddock, Pennsylvania, a working-class town made up of African Americans and whites. Though his protagonist was white (played by Christian Bale), Cooper cast two supporting stars of color: Zoe Saldana (who played Bale's love interest) and Forrest Whitaker. Clearly, not all white writer-directors are incapable of writing characters of color.

A writer's life experience is a single, not total, source. After all, no one in Hollywood expects a writer to have firsthand experience when creating a serial killer character. Writers of fantasy and science fiction must employ their imaginations. For period projects set in the past, writers have to research the setting, the people, the dialect, and so forth. If all stories were based strictly on "Write what you know," entire genres, such as science fiction, fantasy, and horror, would disappear. Consequently, the "Write what you know" excuse is merely a trope that allows white writers to exclude people of color without sanction. As one veteran Latina actor told me: "Latinos get stereotyped because people don't know how to write about us. Not because they're not Latino, but because they don't do their homework. And the only Latinos they know are the service workers."

There are also too many exceptions to the "Write what you know" excuse for it to be true. Danny Strong—a white executive producer and writer on Fox's hip-hop melodrama *Empire*—writes dialogue for black characters based on research. He admitted watching hours of interviews with rapper Kanye West to write dialogue for the black hip-hop moguls in *Empire.*[34] White male writers can even create characters of a different race and gender than themselves. Peter Nowalk, the white male creator of *How to Get Away with Murder* (ABC), credits Viola Davis (the African American female star of his show) as his muse: "Working with her, I've realized how much she's a storyteller at heart. . . . With her performance, she's telling a story. She wants to tell the best story. For me, it elevates my writing. I will forever be a better writer for working with her."[35] Consequently, "write what you know" is an incomplete characterization of the creative process, selectively used by some white writers to justify excluding characters of color. All writers, regardless of race and gender, can recognize the universal human experiences that transcend race and can "do their homework" to properly represent any group with whom they are unfamiliar.

White writers use the "Write what you know" rationale to cover up their own implicit racial biases. In reality, it is a form of colorblind racism that naturalizes racial difference to justify the institutional exclusion of actors of color from film and television. By characterizing people of color as fundamentally different from whites, white writers strip them of their humanity, making it easier to exclude them from complex roles. The "Write what you know" framework facilitates the racial dominance of white-centered projects.

## Blame the Market

A common saying in Hollywood is "It's not a black or white issue, it's a green issue," meaning that profit trumps racial considerations.[36] Hollywood commonly blames racial inequality on market forces, equating white actors with profit and actors from all other groups with risk. A white vice president of development at a film studio explains this rationale:

> When I'm in a meeting about a big film, if the script doesn't call for a black or minority character, it really doesn't cross our minds to put somebody black in it. It's not racism, though I'm sure that's what everyone wants to call it. But all-white movies sell. There's no blacks in *Saving Private Ryan* or *There's Something About Mary*, and they sold at the box office. So there's not a lot of incentive to make changes. It's wrong, but that's the reality.[37]

This ethnocentric idea that the market prefers white actors is a myth that continues to drive funding and casting decisions in Hollywood.

The uncertainty of success fuels Hollywood's culture of racial bias. There is a general belief in Hollywood that actors of color lack the universal appeal to sustain big-budget film and television.[38] Despite having no large-scale evidence, the "blame the market" rationale circulates widely in Hollywood. From film financiers to directors, there is a racist perception that actors of color devalue the market.[39] Director Ridley Scott, in response to critiques of his casting of white actors as Egyptian leads in *Exodus: Gods and Kings* (2014), blamed it on financiers: "I can't mount a film of this budget . . . and say that my lead actor is Mohammad so-and-so from such-and-such. . . . I'm just not going to get it financed."[40] However, an actor's race is not a reliable method of predicting commercial success for films or television shows.[41] In fact, between 70 percent and 75 percent of new television series are cancelled in their first year, making prime-time television a high-risk enterprise irrespective of the racial breakdown of cast members.[42] Consequently, having white stars does not guarantee profit. In fact, the majority of 2014 summer films flopped at the box office despite featuring white male leads. Adjusting for inflation, it was the worst summer box office since 1997.[43] Nonetheless, Hollywood's majority white-male decision makers would rather try and fail with the same (white) formula than take a chance on projects featuring actors of color. As a capital-driven, high-risk industry, Hollywood cultivates racist creative and casting decisions that reproduce the same white male-centered films and shows.

At the heart of Hollywood's "blame the market" argument is an imagined "middle American" audience—characterized as conservative whites residing in the Midwest and watching only white films and shows. This is the "watch what you know" version of the "write what you know" rationale applied to an imagined white audience. It also naturalizes racial prejudice, assuming that whites naturally gravitate toward stories about other whites. Hollywood often references the middle-American audience when casting whites over actors of color. A producer once told a Latino actor that Latinos are "not going to sell in middle America."[44] The trope of the middle American audience can influence how actors of color present themselves. One white female casting director told me that actors of color have to alter their behaviors: "I have black actor friends who have to *be* white on commercial auditions—they have to speak white and move white and think white, and look as white as possible, so that they don't frighten the ad agency's middle America people who have to cast a black person so they get their demographics." For black actors to raise their star power, they have to foster crossover appeal by appearing in projects with predominantly white casts, which receive higher funding and wider distribution.[45] White actors do not face the same pressures. Forcing actors of color to fit into white behavioral expectations further solidifies white cultural dominance in Hollywood.

Hollywood fails to acknowledge that any audience preferences for white male protagonists are "socially constructed choices based in part on the industry's history of discrimination and stereotyping in casting."[46] The very idea that audiences will not accept stories about people outside their own social identifiers (for example, race, ethnicity, gender, sexuality, class) disregards Hollywood's power to shape tastes. Any preferences for white male protagonists must be attributed, at least partly, to the fact that audiences have never or rarely been offered any alternatives.[47] One study of white moviegoers found that "frequent movie viewers preferred White casts to Black casts . . . but light movie viewers showed no such preference."[48] This shows that audiences' preferences for all-white casts actually come from watching films and not from preexisting racial inclinations.[49] At the same time, white audiences' preferences are no longer racially homogenous. White audiences increasingly consume shows featuring actors of color. For example, *Fresh Off the Boat*, with its all-Asian American cast, has a 60 percent white audience base.[50]

Furthermore, the idea of a white market disregards audiences of color. As audience demographics and preferences change, Hollywood must reevaluate who the intended market is. Forty-three percent of millennials (twenty to thirty-five years old, as of 2016) are nonwhite, the highest share of any current or previous generation.[51] By 2043, whites will no longer make up a majority of the overall US population.[52] The imagined middle-American audience no longer exists. Middle America is increasingly diverse, with more than a quarter of the population made up of nonwhite residents. As Adam Moore told me, "There are always going to be people who say, 'Well that's not going to play in Peoria' but I think people's understanding of what Peoria looks like is outdated. I don't think it looks like what [they] think it looks like." Peoria, Illinois, is often the referenced location of an imagined middle-American audience. However, present-day Peoria is more than a quarter nonwhite.[53]

In fact, people of color are the biggest media consumers—exceeding white audiences. In 2014, people of color purchased 44 percent of domestically sold movie tickets.[54] African Americans watch more television than does any other racial group: nearly 200 hours per month, or roughly 60 more hours than the total audience, according to Nielsen.[55] Latinos are more likely than any other ethnic group to go to movies, and are growing in their annual ticket purchases. This may be a continued trend, considering that the market share of white moviegoers declined from 2009 to 2013, while the share of Latino moviegoers increased over the same period.[56] Asian Americans use the Internet and download movies more than any other racial group.[57] All of these numbers will only increase as US demographics shift from a majority white country to one populated primarily by people of color.

Audiences of color already propel the success of diverse projects. Films and television shows with casts and writers that match the nation's racial and ethnic diversity are likely to see higher box office returns and ratings.[58] The financial success of racially diverse franchises such as *The Fast and the Furious* films counters Hollywood's traditional view that actors of color are not bankable stars. The film *Fast and Furious 6* (2013), directed by Taiwanese American director Justin Lin, did particularly well among Latinos, who comprised 32 percent of the audience.[59] After only seventeen days in theaters, *Furious 7* (2015) became Universal Studio's first film to cross the $1 billion mark in its initial theatrical release.[60] Directed by James

Wan (an Australian director of Malaysian Chinese descent), *Furious 7* featured a diverse cast, including Dwayne Johnson and Michelle Rodriguez. One study of 5,438 domestic films (1997–2007) found that African American films generally outperform other types of films at the North American box office.[61] Furthermore, according to another study, "return on investment for white films in the domestic market" is "much lower than that of black films, for which revenues significantly exceeds the cost of production."[62] In 2015, three very different African American–led films (*Straight Outta Compton, The War Room*, and *The Perfect Guy*) topped the US box office for five consecutive weeks.[63] This proves that actors of color-led films can beat out white-led films at the box office. Furthermore, the international film market, with growth coming mainly out of Asia and Latin America, makes up nearly 70 percent of movie studios' annual box office revenue.[64] In fact, with an average growth of 34 percent a year, China is on track to surpass the United States as the largest film market by 2017.[65] Already, Chinese investment in Hollywood has led to increased castings of Chinese actors in films such as *Looper* (2012), *Iron Man 3* (2013), and *Transformers: Age of Extinction* (2014).[66]

In television, audiences of color have brought success to shows featuring leads of color, such as ABC's *Scandal* and *How to Get Away with Murder*, Warner Bros.' *Jane the Virgin*, and Fox's *Empire*. All of these shows have significant proportions of African American viewers (*Scandal* at 37 percent, *How to Get Away with Murder* at 32 percent, *Jane the Virgin* at 19 percent, and *Empire* at a whopping 61 percent).[67] Audiences of color demonstrate a clear preference for shows featuring people of color. The largest percentage of viewers of color tuned into the Academy Awards in "years when the most nominees of color and films featuring protagonists of color were in contention" and tuned out in the years with the least diversity.[68]

Despite evidence of success, when a single project or a handful of projects with leads of color fails financially, decision makers extrapolate the failure to the entire racial group. Despite debuting as the highest-rated new series, *All-American Girl*—the first prime-time Asian American sitcom on a broadcast television network (1994–1995)—was cancelled after the first season.[69] Broadcast networks did not take a chance on another Asian American sitcom for another twenty years. In contrast, when white male-led projects fail, the blame is attributed to factors other than their race and gender. Hollywood is also more likely to support white-led projects even if they have a rocky start. Case in point, the television series *Seinfeld* (NBC, 1990–1998) was renewed for a total of nine seasons despite low viewership in the first four seasons.[70] The differential racial treatment is based on prejudice rather than rigorous research.

Hollywood also fails to consider how racial disparities in film funding, distribution, and promotion can doom projects featuring actors of color. Because studios and networks doubt the ability of projects starring actors of color to succeed, they invest less money in funding and promoting them, thereby dooming many to failure. African American director Ava DuVernay describes "a fundamental disrespect inherent in the distribution and amplification of films," resulting in "cinema segregation in how films are seen and not seen."[71] This is what happened to Tina Mabry, whose film (*Mississippi Damned*) was rejected by sales reps who told her the market could not support two black films when her film premiered the day after Lee Daniels's *Precious*.[72] The inability to see films beyond the race of the filmmakers and actors demonstrates the racist myopia of Hollywood decision makers. The misguided belief that projects starring people of color do not make money prevents them from getting funded, made, or even properly distributed. As Oscar-winning actor Octavia Spencer says:

> There are so few roles out there. And even if it is a film that could be led by a black actress, how many times is that film going to get funded? Let's just be real. But it's not just black people. It's Asians, it's Hispanic people if you're not Selma Hayek. . . . The fact that *Think Like a Man* made so much money last year—over $100 million—but got very limited worldwide distribution is a problem.[73]

There is a long-standing belief that films and television shows starring actors of color do not sell overseas. *Think Like a Man* (2012) was cancelled in France for fear that a film that "lacked diversity" (because of its nearly all-black cast) would not sell, though other US films with all-white casts did not prompt the same concerns.[74] However, *Creed* (2015), a film with black leads, sold over one million tickets just two weeks after its opening day in France.[75] *Empire* also built an overseas audience, dispelling Hollywood's staunch belief that shows with black casts cannot sell well internationally.[76] Besides lack of distribution and marketing, distributors may not know how to market a film featuring people of color. Rather than researching target audiences, they rely on racial stereotypes and conflation. For example, New Line Cinema botched the theatrical release and marketing campaign for *Bamboozled*, an art house film, by marketing it instead as a hip-hop gangsta film like *Menace II Society*.[77] The lack of proper distribution and promotion of films leads to lower box office sales and lower profits. Rather than blame actors of color for failing to make money, Hollywood can reevaluate its own distribution and marketing biases.

Even though most Hollywood industry personnel profess to be politically and socially liberal, they remain "steeped in the tacit assumptions of a dominant culture that retains vestiges of prejudice."[78] Implicit bias affects everyone, regardless of political persuasion. Hollywood's confusion over artists of color who share the same race (Yukta Mookhey for Priyanka Chopra on *Nightline*,[79] Gina Rodriguez for America Ferrara in a Golden Globes tweet,[80] and Alan Yang for Kelvin Yu in *the Hollywood Reporter*[81]) is evidence of an industry-wide implicit bias. They simply do not recognize or value actors of color in the same ways they do white actors. Like Americans' unwillingness to pay more than ten dollars for Chinese or Mexican food,[82] Hollywood industry practices are based in racial and cultural biases that have nothing to do with an actors' net worth. By pinning racial bias onto an imagined audience, Hollywood gatekeepers effectively absolve themselves from any prejudicial writing and casting practices. But, as one talent agent explains, "It's not the audience that is the problem. It's the people behind the scenes. It's the head honchos, the big business people."[83] Hollywood's racist system gets perpetuated because the industry refuses to recognize the implicit bias people at all levels harbor and the institutionalized colorblind excuses they perpetuate.

To change the system, Hollywood must reevaluate how it measures merit and stop positing diversity and brilliance as mutually exclusive. Diverse viewpoints generate more innovation than homogenous ones do. As a result, the idea of diversity hires should not be a stigma but an accolade. Colorblind excuses such as a lack of talent of color or market preferences no longer ring true. Projects starring actors of color continue to demonstrate universal appeal by their domestic and global successes. Intentionality in creating, funding, distributing, and publicizing projects led by people of color is both an equal employment issue and a savvy business move.

# 3

# HOLLYWOOD'S TYPECASTING

*Well, a friend of mine, who is an actress, has always said that being typecast is not a bad thing, actually, because it helps you to get roles. But for me . . . being an Asian actor . . . it's a small market. So whenever they wanted an Asian actor, I was the one they called. . . . But the problem is that . . . these roles are very few and far between. So when they cast something else, they never think of Asian actors to fill those roles. So I never get called for . . . the other stuff . . . when they don't specifically say Asian.*

—Raymond Wong

Typecasting is a common practice in Hollywood. From the lowest working actor to the top-paid star, no one is immune. If any actor has starred in a successful film, Hollywood will try to cast that actor in the same kind of role to minimize risk and maximize profits. Over time, the actor may become typecast or be cast in a limited repertoire of roles based on qualities such as race, gender, physical traits, and previous roles.[1] According to a *Complex* magazine's list of

"The 10 Most Typecast Actors of All Time," white actor Christopher Walken is typecast as a "neurotic psychotic," and black actor Samuel L. Jackson is typecast as a "badass."[2] Though a neurotic psychotic is not a race-specific role, a badass can have stereotyped racial connotations linked to the Blaxploitation films of the 1970s—the most famous one being *Sweet Sweetback's Baadasssss Song* (1971).[3] This exemplifies the racial differences in how actors are typecast. Race is invisible for whites but omnipresent for people of color. Constance Wu, star of *Fresh Off the Boat* (ABC), describes this difference:

> I was talking to a friend the other day about HBO's *Togetherness.* I was like, "It's a show about white people." And he said "Oh, come on, they're just people." But if somebody says my show is about Asian American people, nobody bats an eye. If you think about what that says about the normative context of TV, white people are allowed to exist as just people.[4]

The practice of racializing people of color and normalizing whites is common in Hollywood. This mirrors US society, in which racial and ethnic identities are largely optional and symbolic for whites but compulsory for people of color because of persistent racial labels and stereotypes.[5]

Hollywood is one of the few industries in which one can explicitly discriminate based on physical appearance—whether race, height, weight, or just the director's whim. Though people can get cast or rejected based on seemingly random things, typecasting looks different for actors of color and white actors at a structural level. Casting directors often rely on racial stereotypes to cast actors of color but draw upon a broader range of attributes when casting white actors. This limits the types of roles actors of color have access to, resulting in fewer roles overall. It also reduces the opportunities for actors of color to showcase their talent and build their resume, devaluing their worth as potential stars. Furthermore, being typecast based on racial stereotypes leads to a negative work experience for actors of color. Playing a racial stereotype can trigger cultural and racial traumas that actors of color experience in their everyday lives. An actor of color might play a foreigner stereotype on set and then be told on the drive home to "go back to your country." Encounters with everyday racism, reinforced by institutional racism, place actors of color at greater emotional risk when typecast.

Many actors of color are aware of how racism blurs the boundaries between public and private spheres. Korean American actor John Cho makes this connection between his personal and professional life: "I experienced racism, and in my professional life I try to take roles (and have always tried to take roles) that don't fall within the parameters of any Asian stereotype."[6] In contrast, white actors do not face the same blurring of distinctions between professional and private lives when typecast. In this chapter, I outline the racial differences in how actors experience typecasting vis-à-vis career options, emotional consequences, and burden of representation.

## Options versus Limitations

There is a racial bias in Hollywood that allows white actors to play different characters but limits actors of color to stereotypes. Even when typecast, white actors seem to enjoy a greater variety of roles than do actors of color. Several white male actors talked about how various casting directors typecast them differently. Elijah, a white male character actor in his mid-forties, describes having multiple typecasts:

> I guarantee you I am typecast. How? I couldn't tell you. . . . If you ask five casting directors who knew me what they see me as, they would probably say five different things, which is good and bad. . . . There's one woman who will not see me unless the character has a lazy eye. She just won't do it.

Having different typecasts is especially true for white male character actors, who specialize in playing eccentric or unusual people rather than leading roles. In a 2012 *Vanity Fair* magazine feature on "esteemed character actors," white male actors had a diverse range of characters listed—from "a socially stunted man who finds solace in the company of his pet rats" to a "funeral-home proprietor and patriarch."[7] In contrast, the sole actor of color on the list—Latino actor Danny Trejo—had only "knife-throwing assassin" and "dozens of parts as inmates and thugs" next to his photo.[8] Although white actors get typecast based on individual characteristics (for example, "lazy eye"), actors of color get typecast based on preexisting racial stereotypes. For actors of color, individual characteristics make little difference when race is the main trait on which they are judged. Scott, a Chinese American actor in his early thirties, tells me how race trumps all other "types" for Asian American male actors: "The market has not evolved to a sophistication where you can define everything. Asian is just Asian. . . . So Asian American guys, they tend to be lumped in a big pack . . . good-looking Asian, martial art Asian, character Asian." This demonstrates both the reduction of Asian American actors to their race and the overall scarcity of roles available to them.

## Career Boon versus Career Constraint

As a group, actors of color and white actors have divergent views on the effect of typecasting on their careers. White actors are more likely to describe typecasting as a career boon, while actors of color see it as a constraint. Only the white actors in my study saw typecasting as an entrée into the Hollywood industry and a way to sustain their careers. Biff, a stocky white male actor in his fifties who also teaches acting, describes the career benefits of typecasting:

> With typecasting, I used to resent it. I used to hate it and want them to let me try other things. But the irony is now I accept it and I realize that that's the better way to go. And when I teach acting classes, I tell students, "Welcome to being typecast. Trust me. Once you get to a level where you're big enough, you'll be able to demand the other parts. But in the meantime, let them typecast ya. . . . You'll get a lot more jobs in the long run and it'll be better for you."

Other white working actors echoed similar sentiments—they would prefer to play a wide range of characters, but the career benefits of typecasting outweigh the limitations.

In contrast, actors of color experience typecasting as a career constraint. Raymond Wong, the Chinese American male actor in the opening quote for this chapter, sees being typecast in Asian-only roles as a limitation of a small market.[9] Not enough roles are written for most actors of color's type to make it a career boon. Constance Wu, whose breakout role as an immigrant Chinese mother in ABC's *Fresh Off the Boat* has garnered award nominations, describes how her type does not even exist: "I didn't get a lot of accented mothers. . . . But I don't think it's because Hollywood is so open-minded. It's because Hollywood isn't even writing stories about immigrant mothers."[10] Even when actors of color can play racial stereotypes repeatedly, they rarely experience it as a career boost. One Latina actor describes how she feels about being typecast as a maid: "I was building a lovely resume playing 'Maria, the Latina maid.' It is very frustrating to not even be considered for other roles."[11] The Latina maid type is overrepresented on television, with Latina actors portraying 69 percent of all maids. This is nearly 25 percent above the percentage of Latinas among all working maids in the United States.[12] In contrast with their white counterparts, actors of color see typecasting as career constricting rather than career advancing.

## Emotional Consequences of Playing Racial Stereotypes

Hollywood fosters a hostile work environment in which racism is freely sanctioned under the guise of artistry. Because Hollywood generally stereotypes people of color in negative ways—as violent villains, bumbling buffoons, and sexual deviants—actors of color who play them often experience painful emotions. Taija, an African American actor in her late thirties, felt "insulted" when a talent agent labeled her as the "tough street type" within the first minute of meeting her. Similarly, Jennifer, an African American actor in her forties, had an "awful" experience being told how to perform a stereotype:

> I was surprised because when I did the role the first time . . . the director came up to me, and it was so awful. She was like, "Let me just tell you, this lady, she doesn't take her meds, she got an attitude, you know what I'm saying, girlfriend?" That's how she was talking to me! And then she puts up my hand like, give her high five!

The stereotype lens through which gatekeepers view and treat actors of color can limit acting potential, and at its worst, insult the actor. Furthermore, the negative emotional consequences of playing racial stereotypes are unique to actors of color.

Actors of color can also face emotional trauma when challenging racism on set. Allison Young, a Navajo actor, spoke about the emotional pain she and other actors experienced while trying to combat stereotypes on *The Ridiculous Six,* an Adam Sandler movie set:

> When I began doing this film, I had an uneasy feeling inside of me and I felt so conflicted. . . . We talked to the producers about our concerns. They just told us, "If you guys are so sensitive, you

> should leave." I was just standing there and got emotional and teary-eyed. I didn't want to cry but the feeling just came over me. This is supposed to be a comedy that makes you laugh. A film like this should not make someone feel this way.[13]

Actors of color rarely speak up because of the risk to their jobs and reputation. In this case, the producers told them to leave, which confirms the vulnerability and powerlessness actors of color face in challenging racism. Susan, a Chinese American actor in her thirties, also experienced multiple layers of trauma for challenging her character's racist name in a major studio film:

> I did a role in a film where my character was named Chink, and I really detested that 'cause I was called chink as a racial slur growing up and that was really hard. . . . The director said to me, "That's your name. Just embrace it and accept it." And the way he said it to me made me feel like he was so insensitive to how I personally felt about it. . . . As a result, I found myself really feeling very alienated from the crew. . . . I ended up having a really miserable time through that shoot.

Actors of color can experience double trauma when asked to portray stereotyped roles. The first trauma is when they have to embody roles that pivot on racial degradation. Racial slurs injure actors of color; in Susan's case, the act of portraying a "Chink" made her a victim of abuse. The second trauma occurs when decision makers shut actors of color down for speaking up against racism; for example, by accusing them of being too "sensitive" or asking them to "embrace" a racial slur. When producers and directors tactlessly dismiss such complaints, they further disempower actors of color. Because producers and directors control the hiring and firing of actors, actors of color have little power to speak up against racial stereotypes. Consequently, actors of color may have to play many racial stereotypes over their careers, leading to long-term emotional trauma. Oscar winner Rita Moreno describes how playing racial stereotypes exacerbated her depression:

> People always think of me as very strong, like Anita in *West Side Story* and, boy let me tell you, I had my terrible, terrible times and moments of weakness just like everyone else. . . . It was so depressing to me and demeaning to have to put on a buckskin with a feather in my head and play an American Indian girl or a Polynesian girl or an Arabian girl, an East Indian princess—it was only that.[14]

Racial typecasting, over time, can cause long-term emotional distress for actors of color.

Free of racial stereotypes in real life, white actors do not experience racial trauma from typecasting. In fact, white actors in my interviews accepted typecasting with little to no complaint. Dick, a tall, lanky, and bald forty-five-year-old white male actor, told me, "I'm always going to be cast as a weird guy or, you know, the striking or freaky mailman or the security guard. That's kind of my niche, and I don't really have a problem with that." One white male actor played a white buffoon without reservation. Mark, a rotund white male actor in his forties, told me about his role:

> The white authority figure is usually a sort of a pompous functionary. And I think that's the sort of a standard role on black sitcoms. . . . We are doing comedy here, so . . . characters who are supposed to be silly, vain, or being old or whatever . . . there's nothing demeaning about them. . . . I didn't do anything that violated my principles. I think there's something . . . very funny about city council persons.

For Mark, the white buffoon was one of many roles he had access to—a luxury not afforded to many actors of color. At the end of the workday, he could shrug off the white buffoon role and return to his everyday life. Because the white buffoon stereotype did not follow him into the real world, he maintained an emotional boundary between fiction and reality—something actors of color find harder to do with the omnipresence of racial stereotypes.

## Burden of Representation

Actors of color also bear the burden of properly representing their racial group on screen. The cultural trauma borne by communities of color because of historical and ongoing racism is often exacerbated by film and television's promotion of white-centered narratives.[15] Because Hollywood seldom funds and distributes projects that represent people of color in complex ways, the existent storylines typically exclude people of color or feature them only as token characters and stereotypes. Because of this trauma, borne by both actors and audiences of color, there is a collective burden to create and see more positive representations of their groups. Many actors of color believe the roles they play can affect how their groups are perceived in the real world. Puerto Rican American actor Gina Rodriguez says:

> I want Latinas to look at the TV and get confirmation that, yes, we are the doctors, the lawyers, the investment bankers—we encompass every facet of life. And the reason that's important is because little kids look at the screen, as we did when we were growing up, and wonder, where do I fit in? And when you see that you fit in everywhere, you know anything is possible.[16]

Audiences of color reinforce the burden of representation by scrutinizing and critiquing what they perceive as negative presentations of their communities. African American actor Clarence Muse wrote in 1937, "Every week, some Negro writer or citizen takes a crack at our Negro actors in pictures. . . . They seldom praise these artists for good performances but invariably accuse ninety per cent of our actors as 'Uncle Toms.'"[17] The scrutiny of actors of color continues today. Darnell, an African American actor in his late thirties, describes the black community's outrage toward a character he played: "I played a crack head, you know. And after playing that character, a lot of the black community—they just degrade me. You know 'How can you do that?'" Similarly, when Chinese American actor Lisa Chan played a Chinese woman speaking broken English in a political advertisement that ran during the Super Bowl, she received widespread criticism from Asian Americans on social media.[18] In response, she posted a public apology on her Facebook page:

> I am deeply sorry for any pain that the character I portrayed brought to my communities. As a recent college grad who has spent time working to improve communities and empower those without a voice, this role is not in any way representative of who I am. It was absolutely a mistake on my part and one that, over time, I hope can be forgiven.[19]

As the face and body representing racial stereotypes, actors of color get the brunt of the criticism, even if they are not responsible for the content. Given the dearth of nonstereotyped roles for actors of color, most actors of color do not have the luxury of avoiding stereotyped roles altogether. "When you haven't worked for eight months, you are willing to take anything," admitted Japanese American actor Suzy Nakamura.[20] Korean American actor Ken Jeong, when asked about playing Asian Americans stereotypes, answered, "Everyone is looking for a spokesman. . . . I am not a role model, it's about the work."[21] Given the professional constraints faced by actors of color, critiques from the community often add to the emotional burdens they bear when portraying stereotyped roles. Communities of color can help alleviate this burden by placing the onus of change on executives and creators instead of on actors of color.

In contrast, white actors do not experience community pressure to properly represent white people. In fact, even when white actors portray offensive racist images, communities of color tend to target the creators and not the actors. For example, when the CBS television show *How I Met Your Mother* showed three white regular actors in yellowface in 2014, a storm of complaints was launched on Twitter (under #HowIMetYourRacism) against the show and its creators, with very few tweets directed at the actors themselves. The official apology tweet also came from one of the co-creators of *How I Met Your Mother,* not from any of the actors.[22]

Actors of color can internalize the burden of representation, feeling personally responsible for the images they embody on screen. Sidney Poitier described his burden:

> So much was riding on me as one of the first blacks out there. . . . It's been an enormous responsibility. And I accepted it, and I lived in a way that showed how I respected that responsibility. I had to. In order for others to come behind me, there were certain things I had to do.[23]

Actors of color today still bear this racial burden. Maya, an Asian American actor in her late twenties, expressed to me, "You're one of the few Asian people on television, and I feel like I should be educated about certain things and I should be a good representative." Many actors of color feel it is incumbent on them to represent their racial group positively because of their low numbers in Hollywood.

This burden of representation can place additional anxiety, shame, and guilt on actors of color. African American actor Nate Parker describes his frustration and guilt after auditions: "So few of them had integrity. . . . As a black man, you leave auditions not hoping you get the job but wondering how you explain it to your family if you do."[24] Latino actor Luis Antonio Ramos describes his shame watching a negative role he portrayed on television: "When I saw it, it disturbed me. I was in a position where I needed the work. I needed the work at that time, and I had to do it. It broke my heart, and I was glad my mother wasn't alive to see it. That's how I felt about it."[25] Similarly, Crane, an African American male actor in his late forties, recalls to me his emotional trauma in portraying a man who hangs himself:

> The most injurious moment I've ever experienced as an actor. . . . I was blindsided by a part that haunts me to this day. . . . I abhor the hate that ever allowed for one human being to be lynched. I hate the image as it's directly associated with black men particularly. . . . That image in primetime television, to be disseminated for a 300 million American audiences and then travel around the world, eventually be released on DVD, and is eventually purchasable, haunts me. Most injurious moment I've ever experienced as an actor. I hated it. I hated it.

White actors' experiences of typecasting seldom created burdens. The few exceptions they told me about were ethical rather than racial: one white actor refused to do cigarette ads, another refused to do pharmaceutical ads, and one white actor rejected a role in a sexual abstinence video. No white actors felt they represented all white people in their portrayals, and they did not express any racial shame when portraying less savory roles. Korean American Randall Park writes about this racial difference:

> Is the audience laughing because the joke is funny or because I'm speaking with an accent? Are they laughing because I'm a human being in a funny situation or because they think I'm a funny-talking immigrant? I am constantly analyzing through this lens, almost to the point of paranoia. Geesh, white actors never have to go through this sh-t.[26]

Actors of color have unique concerns over the real-life impact of their portrayals on their racial communities.

There is a systemic problem in how typecasting differs for actors of different races. Actors of color face a racially hostile work environment. Unlike typecast roles that white actors can simply put on and take off, racial stereotypes compromise the personal integrity of actors of color. Playing racial stereotypes can trigger racial traumas that actors of color experience in their everyday lives. Hollywood can work toward equality of representation by eliminating racial stereotyping as an industry practice. To do so, the industry can hire creators and decision makers who are intentional about abandoning racist storylines and creating multifaceted portrayals of people of color. On set, directors can consult with actors of color in a collaborative fashion to avoid triggering racial trauma. Eliminating racial stereotypes will help Hollywood provide actors equal access to all roles, irrespective of race.

# 4

# HOLLYWOOD'S DOUBLE BIND

> *People see Julia Roberts or Sandra Bullock in a romantic comedy, but not me. You add race to it, and it became, "Well, she's too Asian," or, "She's too American." I kind of got pushed out of both categories. It's a very strange place to be. You're not Asian enough and then you're not American enough, so it gets really frustrating.*
>
> —Lucy Liu

Actors of color face a double bind in Hollywood. Seen as neither fully American nor fully "ethnic," many actors of color find themselves excluded from both casting categories. Hollywood and US society at large implicitly equate American with white, thereby perceiving some people of color as non-American and foreign.[1] Born and raised in Queens, New York, Lucy Liu faces this double bind despite having an illustrious career. She has starred in film series such as *Charlie's Angels* (2000) and *Kill Bill* (2003) and several hit television shows—from *Ally McBeal* (her debut) to *Elementary*

(CBS), in which she plays Dr. Watson in a reimagined Sherlock Holmes television series. In the opening quote, Liu talks about being caught in a double bind whereby she is both "too Asian" and "too American" for roles.[2] One study found that Americans regard Kate Winslet, a white British actor, as more American than Lucy Liu.[3] This reductive vision of nationality ignores the diversity of racial/ethnic groups, languages, and cultures that make up the United States, effectively erasing people of color from its landscape.

Historically, Hollywood's narrow concept of America has ignored the long-standing presence of people of color in the United States. Korean American actor John Cho says, "What I'm locked out of is American history. There just aren't roles written for Asians in stories that revolve around American history. So you're dealing with that handicap off the bat."[4] Exclusion from so-called American roles not only limits the options for actors of color, but also creates a sense of disempowerment. Latina actor Diane Guerrero expresses her desire for inclusion: "I'm only going for these parts that are just Latinas and I always kind of wanted to say, 'Well I'm an American too' or 'I'm just like everybody else.'"[5] Guerrero, like many actors of color, does not want to be relegated to stereotyped ethnic roles.

Many actors of color not only experience exclusion from American roles, but also from ethnic roles. If actors do not perform roles with stereotyped accents or behaviors, they are deemed not ethnic enough. Speech, in Hollywood, is a major way to mark ethnicity—often in the form of inarticulate or exaggeratedly accented English. Mexican American actor Lupe Ontiveros describes how, in Hollywood, "the thicker and more waddly [the accent] is, the more they like it."[6] The accent often serves as a form of racist humor—blurring race, exaggerated speech, and caricature into a single comedic moment. Consequently, foreign accents are rarely authentic. In fact, Hollywood's typical form of an Asian accent originates from the Charlie Chan character in film and television, which was first performed by white actors in yellowface.[7] Nonetheless, Hollywood's white imagination tends to lump race, ethnicity, and foreign accents together when casting Asian American and Latina/o actors. One Latina actor recounts, "I was told that I was reading my hooker role very 'white.' She said to me, 'You're Spanish or Mexican or whatever you are. We need to hear the accent.'"[8] Asian American actors also face pressures to perform with an accent. Clint, a veteran Japanese American actor in his sixties, recalls how a director told him on the set of a major television show, "Now you speak English but you're sounding too American; could you get an accent?" Jimmy, a Korean American actor in his thirties, describes that it is "common" for gatekeepers to ask him, "Can you do it a little bit more Asian, can you put an accent on top of it?" Actors of color bear the brunt of having their race and ethnicity reduced to stereotyped traits, such as foreign accents. This expectation creates a double standard that white actors do not face. One Asian American female actor explains, "It's funny, you know, with all of my Caucasian friends, they don't walk in asking if they need to do something with an accent. But I always have to do that and ask that question." In the following sections, "Not American Enough" and "Not Ethnic Enough," I further explore how actors of color experience the double bind.

## Not American Enough

Despite having a long historical presence in the United States, many communities of color continue to be perceived as recent arrivals and foreigners. Asian Americans and Latinos are the fastest-growing racial/ethnic groups in the United States because of continued immigration streams and higher birth rates.[9] This rapid rise has stirred nativist and racist sentiments, which can characterize all

Latinos and Asian Americans as foreigners. However, their presence in the United States dates back to before the founding of the country. Latinos were in North America even before the formation of Jamestown in 1607,[10] and the first Asian American immigrants (Filipino sailors) settled in the United States as early as 1763, while the first Chinese and Japanese laborers came in the mid-to-late 1800s.[11] Nonetheless, actors of color are continuously excluded from so-called American roles. Oscar-winning Latina actor Rita Moreno describes playing everything but "American": "I played a lot of little senorita Lolita, conchita Lolita kind of spitfire roles, everything but an American girl. I was the utilitarian ethnic."[12] Similarly, Daniel, a Japanese American actor in his sixties, told me about the barring of older Asian actors from American roles: "My bread and butter is really rich foreign businessmen . . . or really poor immigrants who live in the slums, and maybe they're illegal—one or the other. I never do the all-American Japanese, because . . . as far as the producers think, they're all young—there's no old Japanese American." Despite generations of Latinas/os and Asian Americans in this country, Hollywood continues to represent them as foreigners.

Hollywood gatekeepers often exclude actors of color from so-called American roles based on surnames and appearances. A Latina actor recounts being rejected for an "American mom" role because of her New York accent: "I was sent on a call as an 'American mom' but they said they thought I had an accent. I think because of my name, it was a preconceived notion. I told them, I do have an accent . . . a New York accent! I either have to change my name or change my accent!"[13] Even though the actor had a native New York accent, the gatekeeper read it as foreign, based on stereotyped expectations, possibly because of her surname. Some Latina/o actors have changed their surnames to avoid this bias.[14] One Latino actor who changed his surname told me that, based on his headshot (which had his Spanish surname), casting directors expected him to come in and perform with an accent. He mentioned that these expectations lessened after changing his name. Oscar Isaac, an American actor of Cuban and Guatemalan descent, describes his motivation for dropping his Spanish surname: "Starting out as an actor, you immediately worry about being pigeonholed or typecast. I don't want to just go up for the dead body, the gangster, the *bandolero*, whatever. I don't want to be defined by someone else's idea of what an Oscar Hernández should be playing. So I used my middle name, Isaac, as my last name."[15] Actors in other ethnic groups have also changed their surnames to avoid being called in only for stereotyped roles. After changing their Asian surnames to Anglo surnames, Indian American actor Kal Penn (Kalpen Suresh Modi) and Hapa actor Chloe Bennet (Chloe Wang) both booked more roles—demonstrating the racial discrimination actors of color face in Hollywood.[16]

When actors of color audition for so-called American roles, they may get redirected to foreigner roles instead. One Hapa actor was asked to read for an Asian foreigner role, despite auditioning for another non-Asian-specific role. Similarly, a veteran Latina actor told me that when she auditioned for a McDonald's commercial in English, she was offered the Spanish version. By redirecting Asian American and Latina/o actors to foreign roles, Hollywood binds them to a single type. This limits their career options because accented foreigners are rarely lead roles. The few exceptions are comedic buffoons (e.g., Sofia Vergara's accented character on ABC's *Modern Family* and Constance Wu's accented character on ABC's *Fresh Off the Boat*), whose foreignness is the crux of the humor.

The exclusion from American roles is even more pronounced for actors of color who speak English with authentic foreign accents. Though actors may be expected to talk differently for different roles, actors of color experience greater exclusion from American roles when they speak with a foreign accent. Latina actor Nanda Abella says, "The moment you walk in the audition room, you see the faces when you have an accent. You see how they look at you."[17] Besides being barred from consideration, actors of color can get fired for having accents. Roselyn Sanchez describes how she was cut from the cast of ABC's 2010 pilot of *Cutthroat* because of her accent:

> My worst nightmare just happened. Got let go of the pilot *Cutthroat* for ABC because of my ACCENT. I have spoken about the struggle I have faced because of having an accent, but after 15 years working consistently on hugely successful movies and doing almost five years on a very successful TV show, to be discriminated this way feels awful. I pride myself on being Latina, growing up in Puerto Rico and moving to America to follow a dream, regardless of the way I speak. I'm sad and disgusted.[18]

Puerto Rico is an official US territory, and its residents are US citizens. Despite this, Puerto Rican actors such as Roselyn Sanchez still face exclusion based on their perceived foreignness. As a result, some actors of color attend classes to get rid of their accents. One Argentinean American female actor "pays $90 . . . for 45 minutes with an accent coach who helps her to sound more American," demonstrating the stigma that accents can have on getting American roles.[19] This is problematic because it dismisses the fact that many Americans of color (and white Americans) speak with accents from other countries.

The exclusion from playing American characters can take an emotional toll on actors of color, sometimes stirring them to question and deny their nationalities and ethnicities. Korean American actor and comedian Margaret Cho says, "I really despise being looked on as a foreigner because in a lot of ways maybe I wish I was a foreigner. Then I would have a country."[20] One Latina actor laments how being Hispanic limits her to stereotyped roles: "If I don't see the words 'Maria, a beautiful Hispanic girl from the hood,' I get discouraged. I know that means I'm not going to get a call back. Sometimes I sit in front of the mirror and say, 'I don't want to look Hispanic today.'"[21] Actors of color, trapped within racist typecasts, can endure feelings of self-doubt and even self-hate.

The exclusion of actors of color from American roles is rooted in racism. Whether relegating Latino and Asian American actors to foreigner roles or denying them American roles based on their accents, Hollywood clearly makes it difficult for actors of color to play American characters. White British actors who speak with British English accents have no problems playing American characters. British actor Daniel Day Lewis even won the 2013 best actor Oscar for his portrayal of American president Abraham Lincoln. Hollywood's racial bias is on full display when it casts white foreign actors in American roles over actors of color born and raised in the United States. Such hiring policies in any other career context would violate equal employment laws.

## Not Ethnic Enough

Actors of color also experience exclusion from ethnic roles. Latina actor Eva Longoria describes not being "Latin enough" for certain roles:

> I didn't speak Spanish [growing up]. I'm ninth generation. I mean, I'm as American as apple pie. I'm very proud of my heritage. But I remember moving to L.A. and auditioning and not being Latin enough for certain roles. Some white male casting

> director was dictating what it meant to be Latin. He decided I needed an accent. He decided I should [have] darker-colored skin. The gatekeepers are not usually people of color, so they don't understand you should be looking for way more colors of the rainbow within that one ethnicity.[22]

Hollywood may exclude actors of color from ethnic roles based on skin color, though the standard changes from role to role. This is the case for Latina/o actors whose skin color is either too dark or too light for Latina/o-specific roles. Given that Latinas/os come from a mixed-race background of European, African, and/or indigenous cultures, there is great variation in skin color and racial phenotypes—something Hollywood often fails to capture when casting for Latinas/os. Christina Milian, a Cuban American actor and singer-songwriter, describes how she is not deemed Latina enough, based on her darker skin color: "My agent was saying, 'Okay, we're having trouble. . . . We send her out for Latina roles, but they're looking for fair-skinned or Mexican.' I ended up booking more African American roles. I still to this day have trouble booking a lot of Latina roles just because I'm a brown Latina."[23] At the same time, some Latina/o actors are excluded for being too fair-skinned. For example, one Latina actor says, "They said I had freckles and white skin. They said, 'What kind of Latin girl is going to have freckles, white skin, thin lips, and blond hair?'"[24] Some actors of color experience both types of skin color exclusion, depending on the role. Meera, an Indian American actor in her twenties, describes how her skin color is a deterrent to landing roles: "I have been at auditions where people were, 'You are the best person to audition, but we're not giving you the job.' . . . My skin is too dark, my skin is too light. I've had both of those." None of the white actors I interviewed described skin color as an exclusionary casting factor.

Although foreign accents can prevent actors of color from landing American roles, not having a foreign accent can prevent actors of color from getting ethnic roles. One Latino actor admits, "I've lost out on work because I don't have a Spanish accent."[25] Latina actor America Ferrera describes being asked to "sound more Latino":

> My very first audition ever, I was about 16, and the casting director [for a commercial] said, "Can you do it again but sound more Latino?" I had no idea what she was talking about. "You mean you want me to speak in Spanish?" She's like: "No. Do it in English but just sound more Latino." I genuinely didn't realize until later that she was asking me to speak English with a broken accent. It confused me, because I thought, I am Latino, so isn't this what a Latino sounds like?[26]

Juliette, a Taiwanese American actor in her early thirties, tells me how casting directors have told her she is too "American" for "Asian parts" because she speaks "very standard English." Likewise, Mia, a thirty-something Asian American actor who grew up in Hong Kong, has heard from casting directors that she is "not Asian enough" because of her British accent and "loud and outgoing" personality. For not fitting into the racial stereotype of the quiet and demure Asian who speaks with a stereotyped Asian accent, Mia has lost out on Asian-specific roles.

Hollywood gatekeepers often lack the cultural knowledge to tell the difference between stereotype and reality. Latina/o and Asian American actors commonly witness the inability of Hollywood gatekeepers to distinguish authentic accents. Adrian, a Mexican American actor in his sixties, recalls a time when he was asked to redo his accent: "I got in to the casting director. I was so insulted. . . . I went in, and I did the role, and they go, 'Great job, Adrian. Now, can you do it with a Mexican accent?' And I go, 'I am Mexican!

This is the Mexican accent.'" Similarly, Spencer, a Chinese American male actor in his early thirties, auditioned with a practiced Japanese accent only to find out the casting director wanted a stereotyped Chinese accent:

> I remember going in for a role for a Japanese mafia guy, and this lady [the casting director] wanted a Japanese accent. So I do this accent like Toshiro Mifune, and she's like, "That's not it!" This forty-three-year-old Jewish woman is telling me, "Can you do it again, and this time in a Japanese accent?" . . . So then on a whim, I start thinking, okay, everything funnels back to Chinese, so I start talking like I'm from Hong Kong, with a sort of Cantonese accent, and she goes, "THAT'S IT! That's the Japanese accent I'm looking for!"

By insisting on stereotyped accents, Hollywood gatekeepers strip actors of color of their distinct cultures and languages.

The double bind Asian American and Latino actors experience reflects their positions in the US racial hierarchy. They are neither black nor white, but occupy a nebulous region in between. However, because race is a social construction, the standards by which these two groups are measured are mutable and often subjective. Consequently, the casting process for actors of color is an exercise in racial stereotyping rather than casting for the best actor. Despite being respectively the largest and fastest-growing non-white groups in the United States, Latinas/os and Asian Americans remain Hollywood outsiders. The perception of foreignness and otherness continues to plague native-born generations who grow up speaking, thinking, and acting—for all intents and purposes—American. This sentiment runs throughout anti-immigrant rhetoric and policies in US society. Furthermore, the barring of actors of color from lead roles in Hollywood film and television reflects obstacles they face in society at large. Even as segments of Asian Americans achieve higher educational levels than their white peers, a "bamboo ceiling" prevents them from entering more senior management and leadership ranks.[27]

Persistent racial stereotypes and exclusionary practices keep Latinas/os and Asian Americans from achieving the American dream even as they attempt to assimilate into US culture. This calls into question whether, under the current racial climate, nonwhite groups can truly assimilate into US culture with equal privileges as whites. One way to counter this racial exclusion is to increase the representation of Latinas/os and Asian Americans in a wide range of roles. Actors of color crave authentic roles that move beyond the binary of American versus ethnic. Such binaries prevent people of color from the full breadth of representation afforded to whites. Hollywood can expand its definition of American roles by reimagining them as multicultural rather than white. Rather than fitting people of color into white roles, Hollywood can create roles that represent the multiplicity of cultures that make the United States a diverse nation. By doing so, Hollywood can diminish the perception of Latinas/os, Asian Americans, and other groups of color as perpetual foreigners.

# 5

# SURVIVING HOLLYWOOD

> *I would often get called in to play a very loud, obnoxious—which truth be told I can be loud and obnoxious (laughter). . . . My issue was when it was like a ghetto girl, I didn't think I was good at it. I didn't feel authentic. And so I had insecurities about going in on it, and I just didn't think it looked truthful on me. And then . . . you get to a point where . . . you need to get a job. Stop . . . worrying about what the job is; get a job and then make moves.*
>
> —Retta

Over a decade ago, I began conversations with working actors of color on sets, at coffeehouses, and in their homes. More than ninety interviews later, I remain in awe of their emotional persistence and creative resistance. This chapter focuses on how actors of color manage to survive emotionally in a hostile climate fraught with racist assumptions. They invoke a repertoire of rationales that help them cope with the emotional fallout from playing racial stereotypes. In a National Public Radio segment on how actors navigate stereotypes, African American actor and comedian Retta (best known for her role of Donna Meagle on NBC's *Parks and Recreation*) demonstrates this complex and even contradictory set of coping strategies.[1] She simultaneously distances her "authentic" self from one stereotype and embraces parts of another stereotype as "truth"—all the while having to "get a job." These are what veteran African American actor Diahann Carroll calls "adjustments," or ways for actors of color to reconceptualize stereotyped roles "to stay away from the area of anger and 'What's wrong with me?'"[2] Institutional racism shapes the emotional lives of actors of color as they reconcile personal costs with professional advancement.

## Distancing

To preserve a positive sense of self when confronting stereotyped roles, some actors of color distance themselves from the role. Through emotional, identity, and ability distancing, actors of color avoid emotional burnout from playing negative stereotypes.

### *Emotional Distancing*

When actors of color perform degrading roles, they become vulnerable to negative emotions. Even though the definition of acting is to play a fictional role, popular styles such as method acting require actors to draw on emotions from lived experiences to reproduce a "human truth."[3] To shield themselves emotionally, some actors of color detach themselves from the performance process. Emotional distancing is a common strategy among workers whose jobs require emotional labor. For example, customer service workers who are required to serve people "with a smile" may distance their "real" selves from work to avoid emotional burnout.[4] Similarly, exotic dancers may role-play to create distance between their on-stage and off-stage personas.[5] Likewise, actors of color can use distancing techniques when performing unsavory roles. Some pretend they are someone else and completely remove their own emotions. One Japanese American female actor in her late twenties describes how she likes to "pretend" and not "really feel" stereotyped roles. Likewise, an African American female actor in her early thirties recalls how she played a role "like a tough person" even though she "wasn't feeling tough." One sixty-year-old veteran Asian American male actor admits, "A lot of times, I'm pretending. I'm faking it. A lot of times, I'm giving the white man what it is he wants. I've worked with all the generations. They have these stereotypical ideas of what Asians are. They still want me to play Ching Chong Chinaman." Actors of color can avoid the traumatic trappings of playing stereotypes by distancing themselves emotionally from the role.

Though emotional distancing can help some actors of color cope with playing degrading roles, it is not a foolproof strategy. Coco, a Chinese American female actor in her late thirties with short platinum hair, describes how she tries to distance herself during a performance: "I had to do these very Asian accents . . . so I just kind of did the role-playing thing and pretended like someone just wanted to see a very stereotypical Asian girl. . . . But when you walk out of there, you don't always feel very clean. You kind of feel like a whore." Even though Coco role-played as a way to guard herself emotionally, she could not avoid lingering distress.

### *Identity Distancing*

To preserve a positive sense of self, some actors of color distance their personal identities from stereotyped roles. Because the racial stereotypes they face in Hollywood also exist in society, these actors draw a distinction between who they "really" are and the stereotyped role they play. Though Retta has joked about being "ghetto" on stage,[6] she also distances herself from the term: "My issue was when it was like a ghetto girl, I didn't think I was good at it. I didn't feel authentic. . . . I just didn't think it looked truthful on me."[7] Actors of color may contrast their true traits with the stereotyped ones they put on for the role. Dawn, an African American actor in her early thirties, distinguishes her identity from the stereotyped expectations placed on her during auditions: "I've been told 'You need to be more street' in auditions. And a lot of my [actor] friends have. It means, 'Be more black'—the head-rolling, finger-snapping type character—it's just not who I am." Angel, an African American actor in her early thirties, distances herself from the stereotyped roles her agents sent her out for: "Because my hair was locks, they would send me out on stuff where I was playing welfare moms, homeless people, and you know, all these things that I wasn't familiar with." Henry, a slight forty-seven-year-old African American male and self-described "non-urban" actor, told me how he played a gang leader and was afraid of the "real gang member" extras.

Actors of color may also cite specific characteristics about their culture or their lived backgrounds to distance themselves from stereotyped roles. As early as 1933, Chinese American actor Anna May Wong invoked an elevated racial identity based on history to combat racial stereotypes. She said, "Why is it that the screen Chinese is always the villain? And so crude a villain—murderous, treacherous, a snake in the grass! We are not like that. How could we be, with a civilization that is so many times older than the West?"[8] African American actors also distinguish themselves from "ghetto" stereotypes by invoking their middle-class status. According to scholar Monica White Ndounou, some African Americans have historically adopted "bourgeois attitudes" to "avoid associations of all blacks with folk culture."[9] Vivian, an African American actor in her forties, contrasted her middle-class traits with those of a lower-income "hood" role:

> I remember I auditioned for a movie that took place in the hood. And my acting, my audition was beautiful. But I didn't get it. I said, "I want to know why I didn't get a callback." . . . They said, "Tell Vivian that when she comes back in she's got to be ghetto. Extremely ghetto, organically ghetto, can't see that she is putting it on." . . . I thought that she was trying to say that there was an innate sophistication and elegance about me that's not associated with the hood. . . . That's just me, you know. I grew up in a black sophisticated, middle-class family. And I went to boarding school. And I went to college. And I was around beautiful things.

Similarly, Suzanne, an African American female actor in her mid-fifties told me that Hollywood writers write "ghetto" stereotypes because they "have not met" her church group of all "rich black women." To distance themselves from Hollywood's demeaning and villainous stereotypes, actors of color may invoke status, wealth and civilization.

### *Ability Distancing*

Actors of color may detach themselves from stereotyped roles by claiming a lack of ability. Retta described how she is not "good" at doing the stereotyped sassy black woman voice:

> I was no good. . . . Especially like with voice work. Whenever I got called in for voiceover stuff, it was only to be [a] sassy . . . smart-alec . . . black woman, and sometimes it was written in a way that I didn't feel comfortable reading. I just wasn't good at it . . . So I never got callbacks for that stuff.[10]

By citing her discomfort and lack of skill with the role, Retta distanced herself from the "sassy black woman" stereotype.

Asian American actors may separate themselves from foreigner stereotypes by citing an inability to do "Asian" accents. One twenty-eight-year-old Asian American female actor confessed, "I can't really do Asian accents that well." Similarly, Philip, a thirty-something Asian American male actor, described how he did a "really bad Asian accent" in a fit of anger, and booked the role because the character was supposed to be angry (not because of the accent). By attributing his successful audition to righteous anger, Philip distanced himself from the foreign-accented Asian stereotype to preserve a positive sense of self.

## Obligations: Financial, Familial, Career, and Moral

Racial barriers and the preponderance of stereotypes limit job options for actors of color—forcing some to compromise their morals. Actors of color often have to portray racial stereotypes as a way to survive financially and professionally. African American female actor and Oscar winner Hattie McDaniel reportedly said, "I can be a maid for $7 a week or I can play a maid for $700 a week."[11] Similarly, Tyrone, a sixty-five-year-old African American male actor, describes how a big paycheck can compel him to play a stereotyped film role:

> So many times, they want you hip-hopping, and it's unnecessary. And that takes away from your character. . . . And sometimes the paychecks are so big, you ain't gonna say nothing. And who was it? It was Morgan Freeman. He said that sometimes you do a job script just for the money. And we all will. It just depends on what we need at the time. You turn down a job when you got money.

Although Tyrone expresses his disdain for Hollywood's stereotyped expectations, he sees rejecting them as a financial luxury.

In addition to personal financial obligations, some actors of color describe breadwinner obligations to provide for their family. Bill, an African American male actor in his late fifties, says, "I passed on some [stereotyped] things; not much though. Can't afford to. The real world rears its head. I have two kids." Similarly, Brandon, an Asian American male actor in his thirties, describes how familial and financial pressures made rejecting stereotypes difficult:

> I have a family to support now that I have a kid and I'm married. And I have a mortgage to pay. And I also need to work and stay in the game. It took me six years before that first movie came around. . . . And one of my acting teachers told me, "You're so lucky to even get paid for any kind of acting that you do." And then I stopped turning down stuff—even stuff that was potentially offensive as an Asian American artist.

Some actors of color also play stereotyped roles to survive and advance professionally. Early career actors commonly see stereotyped roles as a "foot in the door," or a necessary step before landing better parts. Mexican American actor Eva Longoria recalls her willingness to play stereotyped roles early on in her career: "We just all wanted to work . . . and we were like, 'Oh, I hope I get waitress No. 4 with the bad accent.'"[12] Recall Retta framing playing stereotypes as a "job" that allows her to "make moves" to better roles.[13] Similarly, Darnell, an African American male actor in his early thirties who has played "crack heads," sees stereotyped roles as stepping stones to better roles:

> Until I get to the point where I can create my own projects . . . I have to play the game. I have to get in the door like Samuel Jackson. He started out playing a lot of gray characters. Now he plays it all, he is *Star Wars*. He's on top. Once you get in the door,

> once they see, once they get to know you. . . . Maybe the next time the casting director is working on something and he'll say, "he is intelligent and . . . he can play a doctor."

Actors of color often see stereotyped roles as a means to an end. Like Tyrone, Darnell cites the career trajectory of an A-list actor (Samuel L. Jackson) to validate his choice. In the same vein, Clint, a sixty-year-old Japanese American male actor who has been working steadily in Hollywood since the mid-1970s, explains that the actor's "job" is to "book the gig," even if the role is stereotypical. He credits his steady career to his "lack of attitude" about playing stereotypes.

Finally, some actors play stereotyped roles as a moral imperative. African American actor and Oscar nominee Dorothy Dandridge once told Sidney Poitier that "[Goldwyn's] going to do this picture with or without me. He will do it with or without you. Now the way I'm thinking, if I can bring some dignity to the role, maybe that's what it needs."[14] Similarly, Tim Dang, artistic director of East West Players, states, "You know it's a terrible, racist role . . . but it is up to you to go and get that part. And you get it and you dignify it and humanize it. The worst thing about it is if you turn it down, and someone else gets it, and they don't give it that dignity and humanity because it's just a job to them."[15] Arthur, a Japanese American actor in his fifties, told me how he entered Hollywood to prove that Asian Americans are "Americans too," even if the "best [he] could do is to be refugee number two on *M*A*S*H*." To survive as professional actors, some actors of color see playing racial stereotypes as financial, familial, career, or moral necessities.

## Neutralization

Actors of color may justify playing stereotypes by finding positive elements in the larger narrative of the film or television show. They may seek out storylines that neutralize their stereotyped character in some way. Some actors of color are willing to play stereotyped roles if the overall project represents their racial groups in a balanced manner. The idea is that a token racial stereotype can have a negative impact on audience perception, but multiple or balanced representations of their racial group will not. Sheila, an African American actor in her forties, says she would only do a "ghetto" role in "an urban setting, and all of the characters are more hip-hop, and it's geared towards a specific audience."[16] In the same vein, Bryan, an African American male actor in his late forties, describes how he was willing to play a "white guy's sidekick" because his character was balanced by a variety of black characters in the project. He says he typically rejects such roles because he does not want to "embarrass myself, my family, or my people." However, because it was an "all-black project" with other roles that had "their own little idiosyncrasy and their ethnicity," Bryan felt he could "be that Uncle Tom." Bryan qualifies his decision by pointing out that if the character were "in an all-white thing and it was just him, it wouldn't have worked the same way 'cause the balance wouldn't have been there." Ultimately, Bryan chooses roles based on "how that character fits into that story and who he is in the context of that story."

Wang, a veteran Chinese American male actor in his mid-forties, seeks a similar racial balance in scripts when playing a potentially stereotypical Asian villain:

> I have no problems playing a bad guy. They're a lot of fun. I have rules, though. . . . Rule number 1 is, if I'm going to be the antagonist or the major nemesis or the bad guy in the film, television, play—it doesn't matter what medium you're talking about—the hero must be Asian or Asian American. Rule number 2 is that there are no Asian or Asian American women victimized. Number 3, there's got to be a balance of good and evil of my race in the script.

These elaborate rationalizations demonstrate a heavy racial burden borne by some actors of color when considering roles and projects. This is seen in Bryan's desire to "not embarrass" his "people" and Wang's carefully conceived "rules" that ensure a balanced representation of Asian Americans.

Actors of color may neutralize stereotyped roles by seeking out projects in which characters of every racial group is exaggerated in some way. Wang describes his logic in playing a racial stereotype in an "equal offender" film:

> You look at these guys and there's not one guy that's real. The black guy that curses all the time . . . and then you got the huge, muscular, dumb white guy . . . and then you get this silent, dangerous Asian guy who says very few words. . . . And you kind of look at these cast of characters, and you'll say, "You cannot possibly be real. If I believe that this Asian guy is real, then something's wrong."

Similarly, Rose, an Asian American actor in her mid-twenties, neutralizes her stereotyped role in a film in which every character is "over the top." She plays a "Korean foreign exchange student cheerleader" who is supposed to speak with a "Long Duck Dong accent" in a film in which "everybody is being made fun of." She sees the film as "commenting on society" in an "intelligent way, even if the humor can be extremely offensive in other ways." Actors of color may believe that the overall message of the film can neutralize stereotypes. Whether this is true in the larger context of cultural representations is up for debate. Because there is a glut of racial stereotypes in popular culture, no matter the degree to which a film is "racially balanced" or satirical, audiences may still process racial stereotypes uncritically.

## Embracement

Actors of color may attempt to negate the stigma attached with playing stereotypes by embracing some or all of it as "truth." By doing so, they ease tensions between their personal identities and the stereotypes they portray. Taiwanese American actor Constance Wu dispels the critique of the Chinese accent as stereotyped:

> In the same way, there are going to be some people who are mad that the character has an accent because, from a Hollywood metric, a Chinese accent is something to be used as humorous fodder. . . . But why are we using their metric? I don't even dignify that metric with a response. I didn't exploit the accent. I based my accent purely on character work and the truth of a real person.[17]

By rejecting the premise of a "Chinese accent" as stereotypical, Constance Wu redefines her accent as based on "the truth of a real person." Similarly, one thirty-year-old Asian American female actor says:

> To me, stereotypes come from some sort of truth. So, that's the truth that you play. You know, it's just unfortunate that you may see a lot of that particular truth out there. And now people think that all Chinese people are smart or all Chinese people are doctors, but there is some truth to that. I mean you go to a hospital, and there are a lot of Asian people.

Some actors of color may draw upon historical truth. Randolph, a Chinese American male actor in his mid-sixties, describes why he is willing to play costumed Chinese characters: "Our people did dress like that and they were proud of it. I bought the costume myself for auditions, and not as Ching Chong, [but as] a proud Chinese person from the old country, from that era." By reframing stereotypes as representative of real life, some actors of color attempt to diffuse the stigma associated with playing stereotypes.

Some actors of color cite their own family members as the basis for their performances. Latina actor Sofia Vergara, when asked whether she felt her character Gloria on *Modern Family* (ABC) was stereotypical, responded:

> I don't know what they mean by a stereotype because I'm not trying to invent anything from it. . . . I read a scene and I think: "Ok, how would my mom and my aunt play this?" And that's how I've created Gloria. I guess they could say my mom and my aunt are the stereotypes [but] that's who they are. They're voluptuous, they're funny, they're full of energy, passionate and that's Gloria.[18]

By citing her own family members as inspiration, Vergara dismisses critiques of her character as a stereotype. In the same vein, Darnell, an African American male actor in his thirties, defends playing a "crack head" role by citing his own family background:

> Because I came from a very dysfunctional upbringing in my life, I tend to play a lot of broken people. My first movie, I played a crack head. After playing that character, many in the black community said that was degrading. But people didn't really realize that my mother was on crack. I like playing gritty characters, I like showing the people reality. And sometimes the reality isn't pretty.[19]

Likewise, Victoria, a Chinese American actor in her early thirties, references her own family when embracing the use of a foreign accent: "It's not like you created it out of nowhere and you're making something up. They speak that way, my mom speaks that way, my dad speaks that way. It's funny and I'm not making fun of them, but it's just reality." By referencing real-life experiences, some actors of color attempt to rebrand stereotypes as truthful.

Some actors of color embrace stereotyped markers as part of their identities or personal histories. Chinese American actor Lucille Soong says, "I have this accent I can't get rid of and I'm wearing a Chinese dress I prefer. I like the image of a Chinese lady."[20] Recall Retta's opening quote in talking about playing the sassy black female stereotype: "Truth be told, I can be loud and obnoxious."[21] Ed, an African American male actor in his late sixties, embraces playing roles in films about "pimps and hos" by stating, "But I *am* these characters," stressing how he's "been there and done that." It is important to note that both Retta and Ed dismiss these same stereotypes in other parts of their interviews. Such contradictions reflect the emotional, ethical, and financial dilemmas actors of color face in playing stereotyped roles.

Actors of color face enormous obstacles in Hollywood. Not only are there fewer roles written for them, but most are stereotyped. To survive the emotional fallout from playing stereotypes, actors of color draw on a variety of rationales. The range of emotional adjustments helps actors of color maintain a positive identity when playing stereotyped roles. In contrast, although some white actors complain about typecasting, none need to distance himself or herself from stereotyped roles or create elaborate rules to choose which stereotyped role to take. This difference in emotion management demonstrates another layer of unrecognized structural racism.

# 6

# CHALLENGING HOLLYWOOD

*I can't expect somebody who lives in a bubble to write about me. But if he does, maybe I can get in there and shine a little truth on it. That's why I keep marching. That's why I keep going out.*

—Suzanne

In a West Hollywood teahouse, I sit across from Suzanne, a slender African American woman in her mid-fifties with rimless glasses and an ebullient aura. An actor for the past thirty years, Suzanne started in the New York theater scene and moved to Los Angeles fourteen years ago. She tells me about a friend who turned down a role in the film *Glory.* He told her, "I don't play slaves, and I didn't like the way they wrote it." Her response to him was "But see, we are black folk, and if we get in there and we communicate with people—not fuss at and complain—if these people have gone this far to write this movie about these black guys, you need to get in there and fix that." Though actors of color must bear emotional burdens as they face racial stereotypes, the same burdens can empower them as change makers. Indian American actor, Mindy Kaling describes her role as an activist: "My role is not just artist. It's also activist because of the way I look. On so many shows and movies, race was a gesture, and in mine it's the premise."[1] Rather than become defeated by the onslaught of inconsequential or stereotyped roles, actors of color such as Suzanne and Mindy Kaling reframe their jobs as opportunities to subvert, redeem and challenge stereotypes.

Even though the mass media transmits racist ideologies, it is not monolithic.[2] Antiracist ideas can contest and alter such transmissions over time. Many actors of color take counter-ideological actions by subverting, resisting, and challenging Hollywood's racial stereotypes. This chapter showcases how actors of color attempt to dismantle—role by role—the stereotypes they encounter while securing work in and outside of Hollywood.

## A Different Take: Modifying Costume, Dialogue, and Behavior

Actors of color contest stereotypes by altering the visual, audio, and behavioral markers of stereotypes. Costumes play a big role in marking stereotypical notions of race. Images of a Mexican man donning a gigantic sombrero or an Asian woman wearing a suggestive kimono immediately conjure up foreign buffoonery and exoticism. By appropriating sombreros and kimonos as stereotyped emblems of race, Hollywood films and television shows rob them of their original cultural and historical meanings. Stereotyped costumes mark characters of color as "other" compared with white protagonists who dress in typical Western clothing. Consequently, by rejecting and altering stereotyped costumes, actors of color can combat a visual aspect of racial stereotyping. One of the earliest examples comes from the late 1920s and early 1930s, when Latino actor Gilbert Roland had a signature costume that defied stereotypes.[3] Though he played secondary roles, Roland frequently donned an unbuttoned shirt, leather wristbands, and a cowboy hat that distinguished him as a matinee idol.[4] However, actors of color also risk losing jobs when they request costume changes. One African American singer and pianist, Hazel Scott, refused to proceed with a musical number in *The Heat's On* (1943) until the studio agreed to change the mammy-style clothes worn by the black female actors. Though she was successful in getting the film's producer to change the costumes, she was labeled "difficult" and struggled to get additional roles in other films.[5]

When challenging stereotyped costuming, actors of color avoid offending gatekeepers by circumventing the topic of racism. Pearl Bailey rejected bandana scarves (traditional headdress of the stereotypical mammy) on the set of *Porgy and Bess* (1959) by arguing, "There is no place in the world where females dress identically—they don't like each other that much."[6] Instead of saying that the scarves were racially offensive, she invoked a stereotype of catty women. Several Asian American actors managed to avoid wearing kimonos and silk robes—costumes that exoticize and fetishize Asian culture—by referencing the storyline rather than racism. Annie, a Japanese American actor in her forties, declined to wear a silk kimono:

> I was doing this one TV show where I was a mom, and I ran a little trinket shop in Chinatown. And they gave me this really stupid thing to wear, and I refused to wear it. I said, "I'm running a store. I work like fourteen hours a day. I'm not going to wear those little silk kimonos and everything." I got my way.

Annie pointed out the absurdity of the costume, based not on its racist representation of Asians but on its implausibility as a storeowner's outfit. By appealing to the occupational rather than racial identity of her character, she managed to secure a costume change without affronting the director.

Similarly, Dick—a Chinese American male actor in his early sixties—asked to change his Fu Manchu costume by explaining to the director, "We're in Virginia in the year 2000. I'm not sure that he would make himself stand out this much. Granted, these robes are really comfortable and I would love as an actor to be able to have a picture taken with these." Rather than stating outright that a Fu Manchu costume is racist, Dick argued that the costume is anachronistic and inappropriate for the location. He further mitigates any threat by complimenting his costume as "comfortable" and picture-worthy. The director agrees and Dick ends up wearing "regular clothes like you would to fit in, like you shop at Sears."

In the same vein, Clint, a veteran Japanese American male actor in his sixties, negotiated a costume change by invoking authenticity. Offered a role of a "Chinese cowboy that spoke like John Wayne," Clint was surprised by the costume of a "queue and a little pillbox hat." He explained to the director that the costume was more a "representation of the Chinese railroad worker" and that a cowboy character would work better in "cowboy boots and a cowboy hat." The director agreed to change the costume. By proposing a costume change as more authentic rather than critiquing the costume as racist, actors of color are better able to mitigate a major stereotype marker.

Actors of color with more star power, or willingness to forfeit the job, can reject stereotyped costumes more openly. As one of the stars of the show, Latina actor Sofia Vergara was able to openly contest the inauthenticity of costumes on the set of ABC's *Modern Family:* "One time we were at a party with Colombians [in a scene], and the Colombians were dressed like Mexicans," Vergara said. "So I went to the writers and was like, 'Colombians don't dress like that.'

Little things like that, but now they're really good about it."[7] Actors of color willing to forfeit the job can also openly reject stereotyped costuming. Native American actor Loren Anthony walked off a movie set partly because the costumes were "supposed to be Apache, but it was really stereotypical and [they] did not look Apache at all [but] more like Comanche."[8] Several Native American actors left the same set as an act of protest against what they perceived as racist representations of Native Americans.[9]

Actors of color also defy stereotypes by altering stereotyped speech and dialogue. Hollywood frequently depicts characters of color as speaking a foreign language or broken English with an exaggerated accent. In contrast with the stereotyped roles they play, actors of color mostly speak standard rather than broken English. In fact, actors of all races typically take diction lessons from vocal coaches or in theater courses to perfect their theatrical English speech. Overall, actors of color prefer to perform roles speaking English with a standard American accent rather than a foreign accent. Latina actor Stephanie Beatriz defines success as not having to play a foreign-accented character on the television series *Brooklyn Nine-Nine* (Fox): "Our parts weren't about us being Latina. It was just who we were. 'Cause that's how I feel in real life. . . . I'm not doing an accent of any kind, I'm playing this great strong character. . . . That felt like a success to me."[10]

Actors of color can subvert stereotyped expectations by showcasing their ability to do different accents. Meera, an Indian American actor in her twenties, describes how she challenges stereotyped presumptions:

> I walk through the door, a lot of times people don't assume I speak English. That's a big typecasting thing. "You mean you don't do a good Indian accent?" Well, no, I can do a French accent. I can

> do a southern accent. I do a really good southern accent. I can do a British accent. I can do these.

Brandon, a Chinese American actor in his late thirties, describes how he switches between accents to subvert the foreigner stereotype:

> There's this one guy in this movie I did . . . the director wanted me to speak in a Chinese accent. And then I was like, "That's pretty funny." At the same time though, I care what the Asian American community thinks. . . . I said, "If he is such a con artist, then he could speak with a black accent and seem like he's just fooling about the Asian accent." The director goes, "I love it!" So it ended up being better. And I was able to change the role from inside.

Brandon draws on the con artist aspect of his character to subvert the Asian accent—a key marker of the foreigner stereotype. However, he does so at the expense of perpetuating another racial stereotype with his "black accent."

Actors of color also invent accents to challenge stereotyped expectations. Scott, a Chinese American actor in his thirties who says he "won't do anything that continues to feed the flames of Asian stereotype," describes developing a "hybrid" Asian accent: "My thing is like this mishmash of like Hong Kong British, American slang thing. The reason I do it is because it's technically not really an Asian accent, yet the whole room of white people laugh to death."[11] Meera, the Indian American actor, also invents a nondescript accent to contest stereotyped assumptions:

> The character was Benita, not a specific ethnicity attached, in my mind anyway, although I'm sure they were like, 'Oh, she's ethnic. Let's bring her in.' Well, I went in there, and I did a cross between this girl I know, Gladys, from Guam, and Latka from *Taxi*. So, that is the character I went in and I did that accent.

> I was like, I'm not doing an Indian accent. . . . And I booked the job because I did that—because there was something I did different.

Actors of color invent accents as a way to preserve personal integrity while fulfilling Hollywood's racist expectation to speak with a strange accent. Even if their efforts do not actually dispel stereotypes (given the inability of Hollywood to discern among authentic, stereotyped, and invented accents), they serve as a coping mechanism for actors playing accented characters.

African American actors also face stereotyped speech, characterized by slang and broken English grammar. To challenge this stereotype, African American actors may alter the grammar to reflect standard speech. Early African American stars Sidney Poitier and Sammy Davis Jr. "sat down and worked out a dialogue system which would be authentic but not offensive to the Negro" for *Porgy and Bess* (1959), including changing "dese," "does," and "dat," to "these," "those," and "that."[12] Similarly Reyna, an African American actor in her late fifties, told me how she changed her dialogue for a popular sketch comedy show in the late 1980s: "I was a bank manager, and they have this character saying 'ain't,' no final g's on her words, and what have you, and I'm like, 'Wait a minute. She's a bank manager.' So I just went through the script and I changed all the 'ain'ts' to 'aren'ts' and put final g's on." Reyna then described how the director was not happy, but the white female star of the show, who agreed that Reyna's dialogue was "too street," supported her.[13] Although this white star supported Reyna, some reject efforts by actors of color to change stereotyped accents and dialogue. For example, a Chinese American actor tried to do a southern accent on a hit television show set in the South, but the white star of the show fought it because she did not want to be upstaged.

Actors of color also challenge dialogue that demeans their racial group. Anita, an African American actor in her early seventies, recalls how she refused to say this dehumanizing line in a film: "Get away from me, you little ugly black monkey." Actors of color also refuse dialogue that elevates white characters at the expense of their own character. Tammy, an African American actor in her thirties, says, "The role that I just did, it's about a hate crime. And in the last scene . . . the director says, 'Well, you know, go on and thank the white female police officer.' I'm like, 'Thank her? Thank her for what? The white woman comes to save the day? No, I'm not going to thank her. My husband is still dead. I'm not going to thank her.'" When Hollywood creates films and television shows about racism, the protagonist more often than not is a white savior of the people of color. By refusing to thank the white female officer, Tammy challenges the white savior trope.

Sometimes challenging stereotypes involves keeping dialogue intact. Renee, an African American actor in her forties, describes how she asked to keep the dialogue of a role originally written for a male character: "The homicide detective was written for a guy, but I believe that the director said, 'Well, bring a couple of women in.' And I got to come in, but I asked them not to change the dialogue 'cause it's like guy talk. I didn't want them to make it like girly. That was really cool, you know, talking like one of the guys." By asking the gatekeepers not to change the "guy talk," Renee successfully contested the gender stereotype that women have to speak differently than men. Actors of color combat a key stereotype marker by defeating foreign accents, broken speech, and racist dialogue. They also disrupt age-old stereotypes by inventing new and unexpected accents and altering grammar or content. By altering stereotyped speech, actors of color challenge Hollywood's racist portrayals.

Hollywood also expects a set of stereotyped behaviors from actors of color. These demands often manifest when casting directors and directors ask actors of color to "be blacker," "be more Latin," or "be more Asian." Actors of color can sidestep racist behavioral requests to "be blacker" by turning the tables on Hollywood gatekeepers. Yvette Nicole Brown, an African American actor, finds "interesting ways" to deal with casting directors who tell her "to be sassy." She asks them, "Can you show me how to do that?," which "stops" them because "they don't want to do a black version of sassy, so then they move on."[14] Actors of color also refuse to perform behaviors that mark a role as a racial stereotype. Dorothy Dandridge changed her character's behavior in *Porgy and Bess* (1959) from a "liquor-guzzlin' slut" to someone more "ladylike" by working with a trainer to move more gracefully.[15] Ed, an African American actor in his late sixties, told me how he refused to perform stereotyped behaviors associated with a pimp: "I didn't play the pimp thing. It wasn't necessary. It wasn't necessary to go to that stereotypical put your hand behind your back and hump your shoulders and wear the big hat and go through the whole, you know, slang thing to pull this off. So the director allowed me to not go there. Not do that."[16]

Actors of color challenge stereotyped expectations by disrupting the director's preconceptions. Gabriel, a Japanese American male actor in his sixties, describes how he refused to perform the subservient foreign Asian stereotype of bowing:

> Well, I played a recurrent Japanese American character on this television show, and one time, this rotating director said, "Okay. And then you'll bow and leave." And I go, "I never bow and leave." He goes, "Why not?" And I go, "Because I'm an American. Do you see Americans bowing and leaving?" And he goes, "Oh, I never thought of that." So then he let that go.

Here, to challenge the stereotype of Asians bowing, Gabriel reminds the director that Asian Americans are Americans, too. By doing so, he challenges the dominant ideology that American signifies only whites.

Actors of color also try to change the overall characterization of a stereotyped role. Bryan, the African American actor we earlier heard describe how he neutralized a stereotyped "Uncle Tom" role, feels that "a lot of the black projects are written by whites, and you have to fix them." He talks about how he changes a stereotyped role originally written by white writers:

> Every time you see a black preacher, he's a buffoon. He's a charlatan. He's a womanizer. He's never really a man of integrity, a man of God. . . . But he's the guy who's trying to serve his community in a situation where he has absolutely no power and he's trying to do it the best way he can. So they write that character in there and they don't realize the integrity of the man until you show it to them. And then they go, "Wow! We didn't see that. That's great."

Fixing characters of color is a common goal for actors of color who work on projects written by whites. It often involves adding dimension to a caricature; in this case, turning a "buffoon" into a "man of integrity."

Similarly, Palani, a veteran Asian American male actor in his sixties, persuaded a writer-director to create a multifaceted version of a Chinaman character. He said to the director:

> Whatever you do, I don't care if you hire me or not, do not make us Chinamen look effeminate, have no political position or have no sense of identity. You have to make this Chinaman, emphasis on the *man*, a China *man*. He's gotta have some balls. If you want me to play a Chinaman, Hop Sing cook, whatever, I don't want to be part of your project.

The director ended up taking Palani's suggestions and the show won several major awards, demonstrating the benefits of creating three-dimensional characters of color. To create complex characters of color, white writers and directors can consult with the actors of color they cast and do more research.

Not every actor of color succeeds in altering stereotyped character behaviors. Latino actor Yancey Arias described how he tried to play a "bad guy" with "heart" on the television show *Medium* (CBS), but had it cut in the final version:

> And they just kept it all the mean stuff that I had to do looking like this maniacal kidnapping killer. And that was my first lesson. "If it ain't on the page, it ain't on the stage." Starve if you have to, but you have to live with that, and that will be forever in somebody's TV, and I have to know that that's out there. I tried to bring something different, and somebody in power said, "No, he can't come out looking heroic. We got to make him the bad guy."[17]

Hollywood creates racist caricatures through stereotyped costuming, dialogue, and behaviors. In general, to successfully challenge these racist markers, actors of color tend to avoid using words such as *stereotype* and *racism*. This is because the industry's colorblind culture makes it difficult for actors of color to openly oppose these markers. If actors do, they risk appearing confrontational or difficult to work with. Instead, actors of color who successfully persuade directors to avoid stereotyped clichés do so by invoking narrative authenticity and other nonracial justifications.

## A Different Race/Gender

White actors have historically played characters of color, but the reverse is seldom true. Nonetheless, given the dearth of characters of color, many actors of color also seek out roles written for other racial groups to increase their job options. Within Hollywood, the Screen Actors Guild–American Federation of Television and Radio Artists (SAG/AFTRA) contractual language encourages producers to cast nondescript roles, or roles "accepted for all performers, regardless of age, sex, ethnicity, disability, race, color, national origin, sexual orientation or gender identity."[18] Yet because there are no consequences for projects that fail to cast diversely, actual hiring practices continue to favor white actors. Even nondescript roles may go to white actors. One veteran Latina actor describes being the only person of color at a casting call for "all ethnicities"—a role she did not end up booking. The casting director not only brought in a majority of white actors for an "all ethnicities" call, but presumably cast a white actor for the part. Hollywood's casting bias is on full display when even "all ethnicities" castings go to white actors.

Actors of color who want to play roles outside their racial/gender group in Hollywood have to intentionally seek them out. Even top A-list actors of color have to push the boundaries to get more and better roles. Chinese American actor Lucy Liu talks about why playing a cross-race and cross-gender version of Dr. Watson on *Sherlock* (CBS) was essential for her survival as an actor of color:

> I can understand why people who are die-hard junkies of Sherlock Holmes and Watson, that they would be less likely to jump on board, and I think that's fine. I would not want to force anyone into having to go in this direction, but, you know, for me, I—my parents are from China . . . so to me, I don't really have an option if I want to be an artist and in this business, in order for me to survive, this is the direction that I have to go in.[19]

To convince *Ally McBeal* showrunner David E. Kelley to let her off the show to play "Alex Munday" in *Charlie's Angels* (2000), Liu said, "Listen, this movie is bigger than anything that I can explain to you right now, it's about creating this vision of an Asian woman as something that is Americana, it's about changing that idea of what an icon is."[20] By going after nontraditional roles, Liu pushed racial, gender, and national boundaries.

Although talent agents can be deterrents to actors auditioning outside their racial/gender category, some do work with actors of color to seek out nontraditional castings. Samuel L. Jackson, an A-list African American male actor, describes how his "creative team" helps him generate opportunities by specifically pursuing nonblack roles: "It's my creative team who know that I'm willing to do any and everything to get a role that I like. They send me scripts that they don't care who it's written for. . . . They just send me anything. They don't look for things that are African American."[21] Similarly, Suzanne—the black female actor I described meeting at the beginning of this chapter—said, "I go in on white girl roles. I told my agent, 'I do not want you to sit around and wait for them to say a woman in my category, black woman, because then I won't have auditions.'" Similarly, Jenny, a Japanese American actor in her thirties, describes how actors must make agents work for them to create nontraditional audition opportunities:

> I mean they [agents] work for you, so they have to do whatever you say. . . . The last audition they sent me out on . . . actually the age was forty to forty-three. I was too young, and. . . . I was there for maybe ten minutes and saw three forty-year-old Caucasian women who probably themselves aren't thinking out of the box, and I got it. And I shot it last week.

Matthew, an African American male actor in his forties, also describes having agents willing to send him out on "everything":

> The agents that I have now, to their praise . . . they try to send me out for everything. Sometimes I'll go there and I'm the only black guy, which is great. I love it when it's that because usually I go in,

> I have no pressure because I don't see any of the guys that I normally see. . . . When I'm the only black guy, I just go up and go ahead and do what I do, because they're looking for me or they're not. And more times than not, I get the job.

Some actors of color believe there is less competition if they are the only persons of color in the audition room. They feel that they may stand out and get noticed in ways they do not in race-specific auditions. Similarly, Coco, the Chinese American female actor with short blonde hair, told me her "agents kind of got creative and started admitting [her] as a blonde for a role" and she would book them based on the novelty of having an Asian blonde. By sending Coco out for blonde roles, the agents subtly challenge the stereotype of the white blonde. The fact that she is able to book some blonde roles demonstrates that some Hollywood casting directors are open to nontraditional casting. Actors of color at all career levels must seek roles outside their racial/ethnic groups to increase the quantity and quality of their work.

To access more roles, actors of color who can pass for white may do so by hiding or changing their ethnic surnames. Famous actors who changed their Spanish names include Rita Hayworth (born Margarita Carmen Cansino) and Martin Sheen (born Ramón Antonio Gerardo Estévez). According to Blanca Valdez, who runs an Hispanic casting agency in Los Angeles, some actors with Latina/o surnames who look white only put their first name on their casting photographs so they will be considered for white roles.[22] One Latino actor who changed his surname explains his motivation: "It was not about hiding my ethnicity. It was that if before you ever enter the door, all they see is a black and white picture of you where they can't tell skin tone. . . . They can't tell your voice because they haven't talked to you. But they see Rodriguez at the bottom, and a whole bunch of assumptions start being made." As mentioned, Oscar Isaac, Kal Penn, and Chloe Bennet all anglicized their names to increase their role options. To avoid being pigeonholed into stereotyped roles, actors of color may change their names to be considered for white roles. Though changing surnames may help some actors of color gain access to white roles, this strategy is less viable for actors of color whose skin color and racial phenotypes mark them as nonwhite. Furthermore, the goal is to eliminate systemic surname discrimination, not to anglicize ethnic surnames.

Female actors of color also cross gender lines by auditioning for male roles. Debbie, a Japanese American actor in her thirties, describes how her agency of nine years has worked with her to audition for roles written for men:

> The first audition they sent me out on was a series on television. And there's a role for a lawyer that wasn't gender specific, it was just this guy named Alan. And so I went to the audition, and I remember thinking, "What did I do?" I felt so stupid because it was all Asian men, and anyway, I got it! And they liked me so much they brought me back. But that was my first basically recurring character on the show.

Although many actors of color describe actively pushing their agents to submit them for roles outside their race and gender, only some experience success. The key is to find open-minded agents willing to traverse the color and gender lines. Actors also have to ask their agents, up front, to submit them for roles of all racial and gender categories.

Actors of color can also challenge racial assumptions by going after roles that call for "American." Given that actors of color, particularly Asian Americans and Latinos, are usually typed as foreigners, casting directors rarely consider them for all-American roles. Chinese American actor and Tony Award winner B. D. Wong challenges this assumption:

> Casting calls would say "All-American-boy" and I would show up. I'd make them deal with it, I'd make them say it. "Well, what we actually meant was a blonde person." That is what they meant. I knew that's what they meant. Everyone knew that's what they meant. And I was stupid enough to go in there and call them out on it . . . if only to create a sense of conversation about it.[23]

Even in voiceover work, when an actor's race is not visible on camera, actors of color may have to fight to do American voices. Fiona, a fifty-something Chinese American voice actor conversant in multiple languages (for example, Chinese, Japanese, Czech, German, and Dutch) has pushed hard to do American voices:

> In terms of looping,[24] a lot of my . . . Chinese American friends will go in and they'll just do the Chinese. . . . So they'll say, "Chinese up," and then the Chinese will get up and do whatever it is. And then they'll say, "Americans up," and I jump up. Everybody looks at me. None of the white people can say anything to me because they don't want to be rude, and then when they start looping, I'm looping, too. And then they go, "Oh, she can do the regular stuff." And then my Chinese actor friends are saying, "You know, you're making more work for us. Because usually when they call us in, we're done in a couple of hours and it's a short day." And I said, "But if you don't do the English stuff, they're not going to know that you can do it." And one actress said to me, "They're not going to hire you anyway. They're going to hire white people to do that." And I said, "Why? They can hire me. I can do it. I was born here. I can do what they can do." . . . Unless I show them what I can do, they're not going to hire

> me . . . twenty years later, I work every week, and [other Chinese actors] don't. They work twice a year.

Voice actors of color still face racial and ethnic barriers despite the fact that they are heard but not seen. Fiona's willingness to challenge the status quo of who can do American voices pays off in additional work. This is an effective strategy because Hollywood gatekeepers can easily diversify their casts by hiring actors of color to do a variety of voices, including American. This challenges racial dominance by forcing casting directors to consider actors of color for roles long dominated by whites. By pursuing and securing roles outside their racial/gender category, actors of color advocate not only for equal employment opportunities but for a more inclusive representation of all racial and ethnic groups in Hollywood.

The downside of colorblind casting is that actors of color are often forced to fit into a white norm. Even when cast in nonracially specific roles, actors of color are expected to "input their cultural difference and output a standardized form of whiteness."[25] This is related to the market dynamics myth that white audiences will not tune into shows or buy tickets to see projects featuring people of color, and therefore such projects must have crossover appeal, which effectively eliminates worldviews and cultures outside the white norm. Consequently, colorblind casting can still limit actors of color by erasing anything that alludes to their race or ethnicity. Aasif Mandvi sums this tension up well:

> You're either, on the one hand, Orientalized in this stereotypical way that is a cartoon of your culture or ethnicity; and on the other hand, the culture and ethnicity is completely ignored and they just write a character for a white guy and they just slot in a brown guy or an Asian guy . . . without changing any of the vernacular or any of the specifics of that character.[26]

Consequently, even as colorblind casting allows some actors of color to land more roles, it fails to change the system that excludes actors of color in the first place.[27] The better solution is to create roles and storylines that can showcase the cultural specificity of people of color in complex ways.

## A Different Role: Rejecting Stereotypes

Actors of color can reject roles as an act of protest. Rejecting stereotyped roles can be a source of personal empowerment. Sidney Poitier, a pioneer African American film and stage actor, describes this power to reject stereotyped roles: "I was not in control of the kinds of films I would be offered, but I was totally in control of the kinds of films I would do. So I came to the mix with that power—the power to say, 'No, I will not do that.'"[28] For many actors of color, this is a financial luxury. Consequently, some wait until they have amassed enough savings. One Chinese American male actor in his thirties explained that he had finally saved enough "screw-you money" so he could say, "Screw you, I don't need this job."

Historically, some actors of color have rejected demeaning stereotypes to preserve their dignity. Latina actor Dolores Del Rio reportedly turned down the part of a cantina girl in *The Broken Wing* (1932) because she found it too denigrating.[29] Anna May Wong rejected MGM's offer for her to play the concubine Lotus—after being denied the lead role, O-lan—in *The Good Earth* (1937). Wong explains her decision: "I won't play the part. If you let me play O-lan, I'll be very glad. But you're asking me—with Chinese blood—to do the only unsympathetic role in the picture, featuring an all-American cast portraying Chinese characters."[30] Frank, an African American male actor in his sixties, tells me how he rejected a demeaning role:

> I passed on it. . . . I'd been offered the role. It just was idiotic. It was diminishing. Playing a nigger in the sense of that bad word, perpetuating stereotypes where they have no redeeming qualities, and I don't want to do that. . . . It was a musician that was an abuser. He abused women. He abused himself. Had no respect for anything. There are people like that, but I'm not going to play them.

Rejection is an act of protest against the racist portrayals of people of color.

Actors of color have also rejected racist joke roles. Albert, a Korea American actor in his early forties, refused to audition for the role of an Asian businessman guy is ridiculed for his race:

> The series regular has one of those rush headaches, like when you swallow ice cream. And he's like this [pulls back the sides of his head until his eyes become slanted], making these sounds that could sound like he's making fun of Asians . . . I wasn't interested in auditioning for it . . . because I didn't think it was funny. I think I would have felt slighted if I was an audience member watching a show like that. And my agent totally agreed.

Some actors of color refuse to perform to stereotyped expectations during auditions, forfeiting the role. Arthur, a Japanese American actor in his fifties, tells me how he refused to do a stereotyped accent during an audition:

> I auditioned for a film. I was playing a shadowy figure who was interrogating somebody. They said, "Okay, can you do it with an accent? What are you?" And they're not even actually supposed to ask nationalities. That's against equal employment regulations. So I was like, "I'm Japanese." They asked if I could do a Japanese accent. Ah shit. So I did one, and they said, "It doesn't sound

> Japanese." They wanted something heavier, thicker, and I said that was the most I could do. The reality was, I could do a much better one, but I didn't want to because I knew what they wanted. And I didn't want to give them what they wanted because I was afraid if I gave them what they wanted, I'd get the part, and then I'd have take it and go "maybe I could change it when I get on the set," which is like, you're always fooling yourself if you believe that. Unless you're a star, you know it's too easy just to give them what they want. So I just wouldn't give it to them because I didn't want the part.

Working actors often have little ability to alter stereotyped roles, which puts them in a quandary about whether or not to play a racial stereotype. Arthur made the decision not to do a stereotyped accent because he did not think he had enough power to change the role on set. Even when Hollywood does not directly violate the civil rights of actors of color by asking about their race and ethnicity (as in Arthur's case), they indirectly do so whenever they ask actors of color to perform racial stereotypes.

Actors of color can also reject role types. African American and Latina actors commonly reject the maid stereotype. Elena, a veteran Latina actor in her sixties, tells me how she refused to audition for a maid role that would have made her invisible:

> I remember once I got a call. They're doing a film: Richard Gere and Diane Lane. Five weeks of work. Wow, great. "They want to see you." "Great, what's the role?" "A maid." "Okay, okay, so tell me about the role." "Well, she takes care of the kids and she's in five scenes" "How many lines?" "Four." "Okay, what is the character's name?" "Guatemalan maid." She's the invisible worker. We can't ignore it. Latinos get stereotyped into this. So, I turned it down.

Similarly, Vivian, an African American actor in her fifties, tells me how she did not audition for a fat, sassy maid character:

> It was a maid. . . . I'm not saying I wouldn't play a maid. I'm just telling you that they wanted a Jamaican woman to play a housekeeper. . . . They just wanted a sassy, broad humor. . . . I mean, there is no chance in hell and you see me come in, tall, regal. I'm not thin, but I'm not fat. I'm not a roly-poly. And I rarely do comedy. . . . You get to a point in your life where you have to spare yourself the pain of it.

Female actors of color, who endure an intersection of racism and sexism, are doubly stereotyped in Hollywood. In the 2013 top-grossing films, Latinas had the highest percentage of partial or full nudity (37.5 percent and 30.2 percent, respectively), compared with all other women actors.[31] Puerto Rican actor Roselyn Sanchez corroborated that "Latinas have this stereotype that we're sex symbols . . . that we walk sexy and [have] this flavor."[32] This objectification of Latinas was on full display when Colombian American actor Sofia Vergara spun on a rotating dais at the televised 2014 Emmy Award show as the academy's president, Bruce Rosenblum, told the audience how they were "giving the viewers something compelling to look at."[33] Gina Rodriguez, a Golden Globe Award–winning Puerto Rican American actor, has rejected the sexualized Latina stereotype in the past, stating, "I'm not some super sexy Latina."[34] Black women also get stereotyped as promiscuous and seductive Jezebels with insatiable sexual appetites.[35] In the top one hundred films of 2008, "Black females were more likely than Black males to be shown in sexually revealing attire, partially naked, and physically beautiful."[36] Dawn, an African American actor in her twenties, refused to audition for a character named Skank Ho Number One. Another African American female actor in her late thirties told me she rejected a Hoochie Mama role.

Asian Americans face sexually deviant stereotypes in the Yellow Peril and Dragon Lady. The earliest cinematic representation of the sexual deviant Asian was Sessue Hayakawa's character who branded a white woman in *The Cheat* (1915). Pam, a Japanese American actor in her mid-fifties, describes why she rejected a project that represented Asians as sexual deviants:

> There was a story about a Japanese man with the impulse to grope little girls. There was something about the story and the relationship between the husband and wife that I just felt was sexually exploitive. I was going to play the wife, and that just made me uneasy. The characters are written by non-Asians and they're trying to exploit some sort of preconception about Asians and their culture, how the West likes to view the East. It's a very ethnocentric kind of perspective.

Despite facing both racial and gender stereotyping, some female actors of color assert their power by rejecting exploitative roles.

Actors of color can also reject roles as a form of advocacy. When confronting stereotyped roles, actors of color are uniquely concerned about the negative impact of how their racial group is perceived as a whole. Although actors of color can feel bogged down by the burden of representation, they can also feel empowered when they reject racist roles. The burden of representation is, as stated by Warrington Hudlin, cofounder and president of the Black Filmmaker Foundation, both an "opportunity" and an "obstacle" for actors of color in a "racially antagonistic world."[37] Gina Rodriguez describes her rationale for rejecting a starring role in the cable television show *Devious Maids:* "You know, being a maid is fantastic. . . . I have many family members that have fed many of their families on doing that job, but there are other stories that need to be told. . . . I think that the media is a venue to educate and teach our next generation."[38]

Similarly, Asian American actor Maggie Q feels that when actors of color "get roles that are stereotypical and do not push our cause or further our image in media and in entertainment, it's [their] responsibility to turn those things down."[39] In the same vein, Korean American male actor John Cho explains why he declined doing a role with an accent: "I don't want to do this role in a kid's comedy, with an accent, because I don't want young people laughing at an accent inadvertently . . . for me it was important that someone understood where I was coming from politically, as far as representation of Asian Americans."[40] Some actors of color reject roles to support their respective racial communities. They feel a sense of responsibility to walk away from stereotypes. Although not all actors of color think they can walk away from money, some feel a particular representational burden to reject racially demeaning roles.

Suzanne, the black female actor I described meeting at the beginning of this chapter, rejects roles that make her feel like a racist propaganda prop:

> I've turned down roles where I had to play parts where I glorify Bush. I'm not going to be the one to say fabulous things about him even in a movie. I'm not going to be the one to give power to that kind of propaganda. They use a person like me who's very clear about what she's saying to speak about how it's important that we abolish affirmative action. I've turned that down. You see, that's a trick. Have a truthful person talk about that, and you persuade thousands of people one night. "Even that black woman said so. Even that black lawyer." Sometimes the only contact people have with people like me is through the TV. . . . We don't need any more misrepresentations, and I certainly don't want to go against my own beliefs.

Suzanne understands that audiences may extrapolate ideas about a racial group from watching television. Consequently, she rejects roles that she feels can misrepresent African Americans in propagandistic ways.

Actors of color can also collectively reject stereotyped roles, resulting in a larger impact. In May 2015, a dozen Native American actors left the set of Adam Sandler's Netflix production *The Ridiculous Six* because "the satirical western's script repeatedly insulted native women and elders and grossly misrepresented Apache culture."[41] The actors garnered more media press by walking off together. By rejecting stereotyped roles, actors of color take a stance against the exploitation and degradation of people of color in Hollywood film and television. Actors of color can reject roles as a way to assert a modicum of power over a system that confines them to narrow stereotypes.

## A Different World: Panethnic Theaters, Independent Films, and Web TV/YouTube

Hollywood's paucity of roles and endless string of stereotypes force actors of color to seek roles outside of the system. For many actors of color, true empowerment comes from doing projects written and directed by co-ethnics that recenter the stories on their own racial communities. In this section, I discuss how actors of color use panethnic theaters, independent films, and Web videos to showcase their talent and tell their stories.

### *Panethnic Theaters*

Given Hollywood's racist portrayals and exclusion of artists of color, panethnic theaters have served as a sanctuary for artists of color to create, perform, and serve their communities through their art.

This was the aim of panethnic theaters as early as 1926, when W.E.B. Du Bois described, in the pamphlet of the Krigwa Players Little Negro Theater, how "plays of a real Negro theatre" must be "*about us*" and "*by us*."[42] Throughout the twentieth century, panethnic theaters continued this pattern of empowering artists and communities of color. The Negro Ensemble Company was cofounded in 1967 by playwright Douglas Turner Ward, producer/actor Robert Hooks, and theater manager Gerald Krone in New York City.[43] Acclaimed alumni include Angela Bassett, Laurence Fishburne, Phylicia Rashad, Samuel L. Jackson, and Denzel Washington.[44] Its 1972 production of *The River Negro* went to Broadway and won the Tony Award for Best Play.[45]

The first Chicana/o theater company, El Teatro Campesino, was formed by Luis Valdez in 1965 to organize farm workers with Cesar Chavez in California's Central Valley.[46] What began as a theatrical movement dramatizing the Chicana/o community's political and cultural concerns evolved into professional forays into Broadway and Hollywood.[47] El Teatro Campesino's director, Luis Valdez, went on to make independent films, such as *Zoot Suit* (1981) and *La Bamba* (1987), both of which starred actors of color.

East West Players, the oldest Asian American theater, was founded in 1965 by nine Asian American artists, led by Oscar-nominated Japanese American actor Mako.[48] Located in Los Angeles, California, East West Players continues to advocate on behalf of Asian American actors while providing them a space to play nonstereotyped roles. Clint, a veteran Japanese American male actor in his sixties, describes the opportunities East West Players provided for him early in his career: "East West Players that time '72 to '81 was a very dynamic time because it was like we were pioneers in educating people that we could play all kinds of roles, not only laundry men or warlords . . . and where else can you get the experience to be cast but in your own theater group?" Panethnic theaters continue to showcase works by, about, and starring people of color—serving as training grounds for actors of color.

### *Independent Films*

Actors of color can turn to independent productions to create their own opportunities. While early independent films served to restore cultural and political identity rather than showcase talent, later waves of independent films focused more on narrative storytelling that featured casts of color. Today, independent studios release more domestic films (80 percent in 2014)[49] than the major studios. Consequently, there are more opportunities for actors and filmmakers of color to star in and produce their own projects. Yosh, a Japanese American male actor in his forties, began a production company to create better roles for himself:

> Independent film is changing tremendously. My wife and I started our own production company to make independent films for us as acting vehicles. . . . The same opportunities are not in mainstream Hollywood because nobody creates them. Nobody thinks that that guy could be an Asian guy. Why can't the guy be Asian? Why can't that next-door neighbor be Asian? Why can't the lead guy be an Asian guy?

Actors of color who take larger roles in independent films can do so hoping the exposure will help them break into mainstream Hollywood. Halle Berry's film debut was in a small role in Spike Lee's *Jungle Fever* (1991). The independent film *My Family* (1995) launched the career of then-newcomer Jennifer Lopez, who earned an Independent Spirit Award nomination for best supporting female. Mira Nair's *Bend It Like Beckham* (2002) opened up the career of Indian British female actor Parminder Nagra, who went on to join the cast of *ER* (NBC). The independent film franchise that started with *Harold and Kumar Go to White Castle* (2004, sequels in 2008 and 2011) was not only a commercial success but showcased the talents of Korean American actor John Cho (who went on to star in the rebooted *Star Trek* films, and lead the television series *Selfie* on ABC) and Indian American actor Kal Penn (who went on to star in Fox's *House*). For the average working actor of color, independent films can showcase his or her range of talent to mainstream Hollywood. Taija, an African American female actor in her late thirties, tells me how independent films help working actors of color:

> Independent and student films are not looking for the established actor. So to be able to go in and audition [for a role] that's totally nontraditional and book it, it's great because you can put it on your reel and you can show agents, "Look this is, this is my work. This is what I do. So you can't say that I can only play these types of roles."

In addition to helping actors' careers, independent films provide opportunities for actors of color to tell untold stories about their racial communities. Jeremy Ray Valdez, a Latino actor who stars in *Dreamer* (a 2013 independent film about undocumented students), says, "I'm thankful to the mainstream Hollywood community for all the work I've gotten there, but at the same time, I'm not going to be waiting around for my phone to ring. . . . I have to make films that are about my stories and the stories of my community."[50] Similarly, Kai, a veteran Asian American male actor in his sixties, tells me about the value of independent projects written by Asian Americans: "The roles that I have done that have been of some value to me have been written by Asian Americans—people who know Asian Americans and our contribution to the country and the stories about the unknown people and the unknown faces of Asian

America that have really participated in the growth of this country." In the same way, Chris Rock explains why certain stories about people of color can only be made outside Hollywood:

> The best ones are made outside of the studio system because they're not made with that many white people—maybe one or two, but not a whole system of white people. I couldn't have made *Top Five* at a studio. First of all, no one's going to make a movie with a premise so little and artsy: a star putting out a movie and getting interviewed by a woman from *The New York Times*. I would have had to have three two-hour meetings explaining that black people also read *The New York Times*.[51]

*The Birth of a Nation*—an independent film written, produced, directed by, and starring African American actor Nate Parker—has possibly altered the future landscape of independent films. At the 2016 Sundance festival, Parker landed a record-breaking $17.5 million distribution deal from Fox Searchlight after an all-night bidding war. Netflix had reportedly offered $20 million, driving up the offers exponentially. Parker had spent seven years trying to make this film about the slave rebellion of Nat Turner but was rejected by Hollywood at every turn. He ended up putting in $100,000 of his own money and raising the remainder of the $10 million budget from investors of color such as San Antonio Spurs star Tony Parker and NBA All-Star Michael Finley.[52] Framing independent filmmaking as a form of activism, Nate Parker says:

> As an activist first, I have to ask myself: Am I willing to shrug it off and become active in the complicity of this system, or will I use the only tool I know, which is film, to address those issues? . . . This is my tool, this is my weapon. Nat Turner used an axe. My axe is a camera, and sound equipment, and an incredible crew.[53]

Independent films have served as tools for African American, Asian American and Chicana/o/Latina/o activism since the civil rights movement.[54] *The Birth of a Nation* follows this tradition, but with a much larger financial return and distribution.

Panethnic theaters and independent films have served as sites of empowerment for artists of color to reclaim and reimagine themselves and their community through performance and art. Actors of color continue to participate in these movements because racial inequality and stereotypes still exist in Hollywood. However, because income streams from theater and most independent films typically do not sustain actors of color financially, most continue to navigate mainstream Hollywood films and television for pay, with the hope of catching a professional break. However, with the gap between independent and mainstream films narrowing, and the willingness of streaming services such as Netflix and Amazon to buy independent films, this is an increasingly viable medium for actors and artists of color who want to tell their own stories outside mainstream Hollywood.

### *YouTube and Web Videos*

Performers of color are increasingly turning to the Internet and video-sharing websites such as YouTube to create, control, and distribute original content. Web series creator Michael Ajakawe states,

> There are professionals in Hollywood taking advantage of this low-cost form of entertainment that you can broadcast worldwide. In the past if you were a frustrated writer you would make a short film or even an independent film. Well, today frustrated artists are putting their money into Web series and showing people what they are made of. . . . Webisode producers are covering every aspect of Black life online. African Americans are no longer begging the networks to produce their shows and their ideas.[55]

Having control over the content allows artists of color to defy stereotypes. Japanese American YouTube sensation Ryan Higa states, "It's not a bunch of Kung Fu shows or Asian cooking shows. It's every show you would normally see on any other network. It just so happens that there are Asians in it, and it's not weird. We're playing roles that we want to play, not roles that we're supposed to play."[56] Sidestepping Hollywood's institutional constraints all together, YouTube stars of color can define their own roles. With more than 16.2 million subscribers, Ryan Higa's channel, nigahiga, was the fourth-most-subscribed YouTuber creating original content as of February 2016.[57] With advertiser revenue, Higa can make an estimated annual earning of $95,300 to $1.5 million from YouTube[58] without ever entering a Hollywood studio.

Top YouTube stars such as Ryan Higa are more diverse than their Hollywood counterparts. As of February 2016, five of the top-ten most-subscribed YouTuber channels (featuring original YouTube content) starred at least one person of color—*HolaSoyGerman, Smosh, nigahiga, VanossGaming,* and *Yuya.*[59] Together, they had more than 93.6 million subscribers.[60] Besides being more diverse than Hollywood, YouTube is also rivaling (if not surpassing) mainstream film and television among younger viewers.[61] In fact, 72 percent of millennials (those born between early 1980s and early 2000s) use free online streaming services such as Hulu and YouTube.[62] YouTube stars are also more popular than Hollywood celebrities among US teenagers aged thirteen to eighteen.[63] People of color use the Internet and social media at higher rates than do whites. In 2010, Asian Americans had the highest percentage of Internet users (87 percent), spending an average of eighty hours using the Internet each month.[64] They also viewed 3,600 Web pages monthly, which is a thousand pages more than any other racial group.[65] In 2014, Asian Americans watched and downloaded more movies than any other ethnic segment, with 42 percent of Asian Americans more likely to agree that the Internet is a source of entertainment.[66]

As YouTube grows in prominence, Hollywood is looking at Web videos to find talent. Actors' social media followers and YouTube subscribers translate into a guaranteed audience base. One veteran casting director said, "If it came down to two professional actors, one of whom had great visibility in social media and one who was barely recognizable, we'd go with the one who could get the numbers."[67] Consequently, Web videos can help to catapult actors and YouTube stars of color into mainstream Hollywood. Though Korean American male actor Sung Kang already played ensemble roles in both independent and mainstream films, he got his big break opposite Sylvester Stallone in *Bullet to the Head* (2012) because a producer saw his Web series on YouTube. African American female Web star Issa Rae got Hollywood's attention for her YouTube series *The Mis-Adventures of Awkward Black Girl*, which led to development deals with ABC television and HBO.[68] Rae was featured on the May 2015 cover of *Essence* magazine as part of its "The Game Changers" issue along with television executive producer Shonda Rhimes, film director Ava DuVernay, and others.[69] YouTube stars, as creators and stars of their own shows, are starting to rival traditional Hollywood filmmakers and showrunners.

We are on the cusp of a new era of entertainment—one that can tip the racial balance toward greater equality. Not only have actors of color survived nearly a century of marginalization in mainstream Hollywood, but they are poised for a renaissance with the advent of new media. Their stories of survival and resistance reveal how they push Hollywood's racial boundaries, both in stealth and in plain sight. Their acts of subversion and defiance are reminders that, in spite of overwhelming odds, actors of color can effectively challenge inequality. Never before have there been so many opportunities for artists to create original materials and transmit them to global audiences. Traditional film and television are swimming in a sea of new media choices as the margins close in on the mainstream. Racial diversity is no longer a nice idea, but an inevitability.

# 7

# DIVERSIFYING HOLLYWOOD

*Corporate America long ago signed on to the idea that diversity—besides being a noble goal in itself—is good for business. Companies with diverse workforces consistently outperform their competitors; diversity drives innovation, and workers tend to be happier at companies that value inclusiveness. . . . When you're in the business of telling stories, lacking diversity means you're limited in the sorts of stories you can tell—or even think of telling. . . . Lacking diversity is actually a prime indicator that you're failing to attract the top talent.*

—Gabriel Arana

This is a book about reel inequality—about actors of color struggling to succeed in a racist entertainment industry. Despite showing talent and resilience, actors of color continue to struggle for equal representation in numbers and prominence. Hollywood remains an exclusionary industry punctuated by colorblind racism and perpetuated by white decision makers. At the same time, actors of color have been able to survive and challenge Hollywood's racist culture. Through various coping strategies and subversive acts, actors of color whittle away at the racism that threatens to overwhelm them. However, they cannot overhaul the system on their own. Hollywood must make a full-fledged effort at diversifying its ranks. Diversity and "brilliance" are not mutually exclusive. Hollywood can reconceptualize racial diversity and inclusion not as a compromise, but as a goal.

For Hollywood insiders who only care about the bottom line, I suggest several financial incentives to diversify. Films and shows featuring actors of color are topping box offices as well as television rankings. Hollywood simply cannot afford to ignore an increasingly diverse domestic audience base and growing international market. As an industry, Hollywood also risks stagnation because racially and gender diverse groups are more likely to innovate and create than groups with less diverse members.[1] Finally, studies show that companies employing more people of color and women earn more than those with all white men.[2]

Those of us outside the Hollywood industry also have a stake in its diversity. We live in a media-saturated society that misrepresents its population. Racial stereotypes in film and television contribute to interracial hostilities and mistrust between different groups and to intraracial self-esteem problems within groups. To challenge the behemoth of racist imagery generated by a century of film and television programming, we can demand more counter-images, starting with a wider breadth of roles for actors of color to play. The under- and misrepresentation of actors of color in film and television is a societal problem that necessitates mass intervention on multiple fronts. I begin this concluding chapter with a review of past efforts to achieve diversity in the Hollywood industry and end with a few propositions of my own.

Historically, collective efforts by civil rights organizations, pan-ethnic arts organizations, minority media groups, and actors' guilds have attempted to rectify the exclusion and distortion of actors of color in Hollywood. Though protests (or public demonstrations expressing objection to a course of action) and other organized efforts have not resulted in dramatic and complete change, they have chipped away at the bias. Continued collective actions are essential to combat the gross under- and misrepresentation of actors of color within Hollywood. Historically, civil rights organizations have protested Hollywood's use of images that adversely affect the welfare of racial minorities in the United States. The National Association for the Advancement of Colored People (NAACP), in particular, has a long-standing history of protesting the misrepresentation and exclusion of African Americans in Hollywood using boycotts, bans, and litigation. The NAACP first protested D. W. Griffith's *Birth of a Nation* in 1915, which led to five states and nineteen cities banning the film for its racist portrayals of African Americans and glorification of the Ku Klux Klan.[3] The NAACP also launched a protest against the television show *Amos 'n' Andy*, which was produced from 1951 to 1953 and aired in syndication until 1966.[4] Eventually, CBS agreed to withdraw the series from syndication after five years of litigation.[5]

Efforts to combat racist imagery in Hollywood may vary by time and group. Often, there are contradictory or changing purposes within groups, including disagreements about who or what to protest. For instance, there have been divergent goals within the black community with respect to Hollywood's representations of blacks—with some supporting the integration of actors of color into the white-dominant industry and others wanting to block any image that portrays blacks in a negative light.[6] Within the Hollywood industry, black artists have often seen protests from outside groups as elitist and encroaching upon the precious few jobs to which they have access. In fact, some successful NAACP campaigns against racist imagery in Hollywood led to fewer roles for black actors at the time.[7] For this reason, protests against both the television show *Amos 'n' Andy* and the Blaxploitation films of the 1970s proved controversial within black artistic communities.[8]

Though protests do not always result in immediate victories, they may sow seeds for change. In 1990, the musical *Miss Saigon* elicited a major protest by Asian American theater artists when it cast Jonathan Pryce, a British white actor, in the role of a Eurasian character, which he played in yellowface makeup (prosthetics and bronzer cream). Many Asian American theater artists sought the support of Actor's Equity, the union for theater actors, to bar Pryce from performing.[9] Actor's Equity ultimately ended its protest when *Miss Saigon* threatened to shut down its New York production. Although the protest failed to prevent Pryce from playing the Eurasian role, all actors subsequently cast in that show were Asian Americans.[10]

In 1999, the *Los Angeles Times* reported a nearly all-white primetime television lineup in which none of the twenty-six shows premiering on the major broadcast networks featured an actor of color in a leading role.[11] This prompted a flurry of protests by civil rights organizations such as the NAACP, and industry-themed ethnic organizations such as East West Players.[12] Specifically, the National Council of La Raza organized a protest called a National Brownout, in which they advised their members not to watch television during the week of September 12, 1999.[13] Similarly, the president of the NAACP, Kweisi Mfume, threatened to call a boycott or to take "legal action against the networks' broadcasting licenses" for "violating the 1934 Communications Act."[14] Ultimately, the NAACP, along with various civil rights and arts/industry organizations, formed a national Multi-Ethnic Media, or "Grand," Coalition to tackle the lack of diversity in prime-time television. Some of the major organizations in the coalition were the Brotherhood Crusade; Nosotros, an advocacy group for Latinos in the entertainment industry; Native Americans in Film; and the newly formed Asian Pacific American Media Coalition (APAMC), which included organizations such as the Asian American Justice Center, East West Players, Japanese American Citizens League, Media Action Network for Asian Americans, National Federation of Filipino American Associations, OCA National, and Visual Communications.[15] The Grand Coalition held meetings with the networks that produced a memorandum of understanding with ABC, CBS, Fox, and NBC, requiring each of the four major television networks to institute programs designed to increase diversity both in front of the cameras and behind the scenes.[16] As a result, all four networks hired a vice president of diversity and created programs to boost the hiring of writers, directors, actors, and executives from diverse backgrounds.[17] Furthermore, each of the broadcast television networks adopted diversity initiatives.[18] Despite signing agreements and establishing diversity departments and initiatives, the networks had no specified goals or timetables.[19] And though the Grand Coalition continues to monitor the progress of the networks, change has been sporadic and slow. Nonetheless, though the efforts have not overhauled the system, television looks more racially diverse than previously.

Fast forward to 2014, which has been touted as one of the most diverse years Hollywood has seen. Hollywood awarded its first best picture Oscar to a film that had a director of color—*12 Years a Slave*, directed by black British director Steve McQueen. Both Fox and ABC were on the forefront of diversity among their peers. Around 2010, Fox began framing "diversity as a business imperative" and "shifting the conversation to the need for TV programming that reflects the multicultural reality of today's world to keep younger viewers."[20] The message Fox sent out was that "diversity increases the chance Fox will pick up a new show, promote it, syndicate it, and see it do well with audiences."[21] This came to fruition in fall 2013 with Fox's sleeper hit *Sleepy Hollow*, which featured an African American female lead. In addition, Fox produced *Brooklyn Nine-Nine*, which boasted an incredibly diverse cast because of "race-blind casting" that resulted in "two Latina actresses, one Italian guy, one half-Italian half-Jewish lady, two African American guys, and Andy Samberg."[22] Not only was the cast diverse, but according to one critic, "All the characters have identities that come secondary to their race . . . [and] are given personalities that never once have to pander to stereotypes."[23] In its inaugural season, *Brooklyn Nine-Nine* won two Golden Globe Awards—one for best comedy series and one for Andy Samberg as best actor on a comedy show. Fox's *Empire*, which began airing in 2015, is a great example of how a predominantly black show can be a huge ratings success. Fox's diversity efforts reflect the trend for broadcast networks to move away from the kind of all-white casts they had in 1999.[24] Fox has come a long way since its president, Doug Herzog, dismissed the absence of minorities in 1999 by saying he wanted "the best show on the air."[25] Now Fox's best show is *Empire*.

Similarly, ABC's head of casting, Keli Lee, has invested in finding talent of color. Since 2001, ABC has a Casting Department Talent Showcase that auditions and develops actors of color. Past actors include Oscar-winner Lupita Nyong'o, Carrie Ann Inaba (*Dancing with the Stars*), and ABC television series regulars Jorge Garcia (*LOST*) and Randall Park (*Fresh Off the Boat*). In 2014, I had a chance to ask Randall Park about his experiences with diversity showcases, especially the ABC showcase. He said the ABC showcase helped him "a lot" in his early career because it got him his agent. ABC also houses Shonda Rhimes, whose show *Grey's Anatomy* is the gold standard for diverse and open casting by not specifying any of the characters' ethnicities or surnames.[26] *Scandal*, starring black female actor Kerry Washington, is another of Rhimes's biggest hits. In 2014, ABC added another new drama from showrunner Rhimes—*How to Get Away with Murder*, starring Viola Davis—plus three new sitcoms with casts of color (*blackish, Cristela*, and *Fresh Off the Boat*). *How to Get Away with Murder, blackish*, and *Fresh Off the Boat* were all renewed for a second season in 2014–2015.

CBS also increased its commitment to diversity in 2014, with its top executives stating, "Diversity is our most important issue" at meetings with agencies.[27] They have hosted a sketch comedy showcase for more than ten years, with thirty-two of its actors, including *Jane the Virgin*'s Gina Rodriguez, subsequently landing jobs as series regulars.[28] Industry insiders seem to prefer the CBS showcase because its original sketch comedy bits tend to be "edgier" than bits in other dramatic showcases. Although CBS has cast Halle Berry and Maggie Q as dramatic leads, the network admits it has a "long way to go" in its comedies.[29]

Although broadcast television's 2014–2015 prime-time season appeared to have more casts and leads of color than before, my analysis of the casts reveals that racial disparities have not improved for actors of color as a whole. Whites occupied 72 percent of all regular roles, African Americans 13 percent, Latinos 8 percent, and Asians 5 percent. The majority of television shows still star white actors. Consequently, even when television looks more diverse than ever, the numbers reveal that characters of color have not reached parity with their US population. Furthermore, as networks attempt to diversify, there may be a backlash. Accusations of reverse racism have risen, with critiques that TV networks are trying to fulfill an "ethnic quota."[30] Although studios and networks seem more open to racial diversity, more work remains to be done.

The groundwork for racial diversity has been laid down by civil and media rights groups, yet Hollywood has not been held accountable. Full participation by people of color and women in Hollywood continues to lag behind that of white males, requiring further strategies. A multipronged effort is needed to transform Hollywood film and television. Even if there may be contradictory interests at times between artists and outside groups, efforts to protest stereotypes and to create more roles can complement one another in the larger picture. As long as a steady and effective push for more inclusive hiring is made, protests against racist representations of people of color in film and television can continue without hurting artists of color. Especially in the age of YouTube, multiple platforms of expression are available to artists of color. My proposed strategies include greater oversight by the government, more incentives and programs from Hollywood studios and guilds, and audience activism. I break down my strategies (and list resources) within each of the following sections: (1) institutions, (2) actors of color, and (3) audience members.

## Institutions

Institutions can make the biggest impact on racial equality. Ranging from the government to studios to guilds, institutions can diversify Hollywood's employment and content by compliance pressures, incentives, and establishing responsibility structures.

### *The Government*

Through the Federal Communications Commission (FCC), the government can impose stronger regulations on broadcast television's hiring policies. Given that the 1934 Communications Act contains a nondiscrimination section that "requires cable companies to practice equal opportunity in employment with regard to race, color, religion, national origin, age, and sex," the FCC has a mandate to enforce equal representation.[31] As a result, with licensing and regulatory power over broadcast television, the FCC should exercise the right to bring television studios into alignment with equal employment hiring laws. Research shows that federal affirmative action requirements, which typically lead to the assignment of responsibility for compliance, are effective in increasing racial diversity in the workplace.[32]

The broadcast television networks need a reminder that they are supposed to serve public interests—including how they represent people of color. By underproducing television shows that serve audiences of color, broadcast networks violate the broadcasters' public interest obligations under the Federal Communications Act.[33] The 2014–2015 broadcast television season, despite being touted as one of the most diverse, still hired actors of color below their population percentages overall and cast them in mainly ethnically homogenous shows. White actors populated all other shows in excess of their population proportion. Persistent racial disparity in and of itself should warrant greater regulation on the part of the FCC.[34]

I urge the FCC to formulate, with broadcast and public television stations, five- and ten-year plans that allow broadcast television networks to bring their percentages of actors of color up to population parity for each group. Networks can achieve this through diverse castings within a few shows, but ideally across several shows that showcase people of color (both men and women). If they comply by the fifth year, the FCC can issue tax credits of up to 10 percent of the project's budget and maintain the credit as long as the numbers remain consistent with the overall population percentages. If a network does not comply by the tenth year, then the FCC can withhold licensing from that network or fine the network an established percentage each additional year it does not comply. The same may be done with streaming entertainment services such as Netflix, Amazon Prime, and Hulu because they use the Internet, which the FCC can also regulate.

### *Film Studios and Television Networks*

Studios and networks need to take responsibility for diversifying their ranks. They can establish specific committees, staff positions, and hiring plans dedicated to increasing representation of people of color, which research shows increases racial diversity in the workplace, particularly at the managerial level.[35] By establishing diversity committees, Hollywood can hire staff who demonstrate a track record in creating content for people of color and casting them in varied and complex roles. Director Lexi Alexander splits the types of people doing diversity in Hollywood into two camps: "Film or TV executives who have no understanding of the issue and haven't bothered to educate themselves on what inclusion actually means . . . and real diversity experts who have no internal company support and are drowning in the stormy ocean as their carefree colleagues and superiors hit them in the head with their jet skis."[36] Hollywood needs to hire and support the latter group of "real diversity experts."

Most companies use professional recruiters, and Hollywood can do the same across all ranks. Each studio and network should have at least one designated recruiter for diverse talent behind the scenes and a designated casting director who is trained to find actors of color. In fact, Hollywood should consider hiring antiracist casting directors who specifically cast actors of color in nonstereotyped roles that also honor their racial/ethnic identities in complex ways. Such antiracist casting directors can seek out talent from panethnic and multicultural theater productions as well as digital media spaces such as YouTube. They can advertise job notices and casting calls on Twitter and other social media heavily used by people of color. Studios should also employ a version of the Rooney Rule, according to which football teams must interview people of color during searches for new head coaches and general managers. Hollywood can intentionally invite people of color to interview for studio heads, executives, writers, directors, producers, and actors. Stacey Smith of USC and Spike Lee have both suggested applying the Rooney Rule to Hollywood to hire more women and people of color.[37]

Studios should set hiring goals to bring the numbers of people of color both in front and behind the scenes up to their US population percentage. Research shows that setting specific hiring goals aimed at increasing the number of people of color is one of the most effective ways of diversifying workplaces.[38] To increase the number of people of color in the pipeline, the hiring should occur semiannually or even quarterly. Although many networks host diversity programs and showcases for actors, writers, and directors from underrepresented groups, they do not guarantee jobs at the end of the showcase. Networks can set aside jobs for artists of underrepresented groups at the end of the workshop. This is one way for networks to reach their target numbers of underrepresented groups, if a FCC diversity mandate is set. Current diversity programs require improvement. Because they are not guaranteed a job after their initial pay from a diversity program runs out, "the vast majority of diversity writers are released from their shows," says a Latina writer who did not get hired on her network program.[39] Rather, as Thomas Wong, a graduate of the ABC and Fox programs and a story editor on *Minority Report* (Fox), says, "Hiring diverse writers shouldn't be seen as a burden or an obligation. We bring value. We have a different perspective. Over time, as diverse writers rise through the ranks to become decision makers, it will be a nonissue."[40] Consequently, networks also need to value increasing their staff of color enough to support them beyond the initial hiring period. Furthermore, studios and networks should rethink the name "diversity hire" because a stigma of lower qualifications or free labor is often associated with such labels. Instead, studios and networks can work on rebranding such programs as inclusive and necessary.

Besides hiring, networks and studios can focus on retaining artists of color. They can establish networking and mentoring programs for people of color, which research finds to have a positive effect on retention.[41] They can pair new hires of color with key experienced people. This practice already exists at the showrunner level. ABC mandated that Shonda Rhimes, who had no television showrunner experience prior to her first show, *Grey's Anatomy*, be paired with James Parriott, an experienced showrunner.[42] This practice can be instituted across all ranks and positions. Such pairings do not just benefit the incoming people of color in terms of training and mentorship, but also veterans, who get exposure to fresh perspectives and new ideas. This is an ideal collaboration. By generating inclusive social networks, Hollywood will attract more talent of color. Chris Rock attributes his own success to the willingness of established black actors, such as Eddie Murphy, Keenen Ivory Wayans, and Arsenio Hall, to take "chances" on him.[43] He, in turn, helps develop other black actors, such as Leslie Jones. More people of color in key positions and in the pipeline will accelerate racial inclusion in the industry.

Ideologically, Hollywood needs an overhaul of its racist culture. Creators such as writers, producers, and directors need to think more broadly when creating roles, and talent agencies, casting directors, and studios need to broaden their casting practices. Though research results about the efficacy of implicit bias, cultural awareness, and racial/sexual harassment training have been mixed,[44] Hollywood can bring experts to develop specialized workshops for the creative industry to broaden their imagination and artistry when it comes to race, ethnicity, and gender. In September 2009, the Equal Justice Society organized a panel that included the Writers Guild of America, West, the Screen Actors Guild, the American Values Institute, and the Kirwan Institute to expose creators in the entertainment industry to the concept of implicit bias for the purposes of developing and producing diverse programming.[45] Given the mixed results on the efficacy of implicit bias and antibias training, further study (particularly in the creative fields) is necessary before making future recommendations for the Hollywood industry. Nonetheless, as we enter an increasingly racially diverse and global society, the ability to creatively engage different racial and ethnic groups is essential in Hollywood.

### *Guilds*

Guilds and unions can provide more incentives, such as fee breaks, for studios and networks to hire actors and creators of color (e.g., writers, directors, and producers). One existing incentive from the actor's union SAG-AFTRA is the Diversity-in-Casting Incentive. This incentive allows "low-budget filmmakers" who meet a particular set of criteria that involves employing actors of color and other underrepresented groups to increase the total production cost maximum up to 50 percent, without having to pay actors at higher union rates.[46] This allows productions to save money while also casting more diversely. There is evidence of the success of this program. From 2002 to 2010, the number of projects taking advantage of the incentive increased from 2 percent of low-budget productions to 20 percent.[47] Award-winning films such as *Hustle and*

*Flow* (2005), which also garnered a nomination for best actor Oscar for African American actor Terrance Howard, have made use of this incentive.[48] Howard's career is once again on top, as he stars in the top-rated broadcast network show, *Empire*. Other actors of color who have benefited from this union incentive include Latina female actor Olga Segura, who said, "SAG helps a lot thanks to the Diversity-in-Casting Incentives . . . because it forces us to write our own stories, and it forces producers to promote characters that represent us."[49] Mike Hodge, an African American actor and president of the SAG-AFTRA New York chapter, also praised the Diversity Incentives for financing stories that would otherwise be difficult to tell.[50] SAG-AFTRA can build upon the success of this incentive and extend it to projects of all budget sizes. The fee break system can also be based on meeting the U.S. population percentage baseline, with greater fee breaks as more underrepresented groups are included. Other unions (e.g., Directors Guild of America, Producers Guild of America, and Writers Guild of America) can follow suit and create similar incentives to encourage the hiring of people of color within their ranks.

Overall, raising the numbers of people of color working in the industry is only one piece of the solution. The types of representations must also improve. One study of eighty-eight popular national magazines found that as representations of African Americans in popular magazines increased, stereotyped role-portrayals of African Americans also increased.[51] Consequently, hiring more artists of color is necessary but insufficient in creating inclusive creative content. Guilds can also provide additional fee breaks for shows that feature actors of color in stories about and by people of color. Incentives can encourage studios to go further than just increasing their numbers by finding new stories that counter rather than rehash racial stereotypes.

## Actors of Color

The most prominent programs geared toward actors of color are showcases, in which a select group of actors of color perform sketch comedy, one-act vignettes, or stand-up comedy for invited casting directors, talent agents, managers, and other industry professionals. Television networks, sometimes in collaboration with unions and panethnic arts organizations, run these showcases on an annual basis. I break them down here by networks.

ABC/Disney Television Group runs the ABC Casting Project's Talent Showcase,[52] which, according to its official website, results in 90 percent of showcase actors auditioning for or being cast as a series regular, recurring, or guest role on prime-time and/or daytime television, as well as being cast in film and commercial roles. I attended the Hollywood showcases from 2012 to 2015. Most of the dozen or so participants were African American, Latino, Asian (East and South), or Middle Eastern; one or two were white actors. Several LGBTQ actors and a performer with disabilities have also participated. The participants performed one-act vignettes, either in pairs or groups of three or four, to an audience of talent agents, studio executives, and casting directors from various networks. As I wrote earlier, Randall Park (star of *Fresh Off the Boat*) got his talent agent after performing in this showcase.

CBS has a popular comedy showcase[53] that has the advantage of multiple shows (compared with Disney/ABC's showcase, which only has one), allowing for more eyeballs (i.e., greater attendance by influential gatekeepers and key players in the industry). According to Fern Orenstein, a senior vice president of casting at CBS who serves as producer for the showcase, the showcase sees about "four- or five-hundred casting directors" and "the rest are agents and managers, development executives."[54] I attended one of six scheduled runs of the showcase each year from 2014 to 2016 in Hollywood. A variety of sketches ranged from ones that overtly challenged Hollywood stereotypes (e.g., a musical number in which women of color sang about getting typecast or sexually objectified in Hollywood) to casting actors of color in traditionally white-dominated genres (e.g., a romantic comedy sketch with a Latina and Latino actor portraying restaurant service workers flirting and falling in love). Director Rick Najera said the 2015 showcase had four thousand applicants, half of whom were invited to audition. They selected twenty-one actors, the majority of whom were people of color, for the final showcase. Within a week of the 2016 showcase, CBS's sitcom *Two Broke Girls* had already cast half a dozen of the performers.[55]

NBC has two initiatives for actors. The first is Stand up NBC, which focuses specifically on comedians. According to its website, NBC holds auditions and live showcases for the top diverse talent in three to five cities it identifies around the country: "At the end of the search a handful of comedians are brought back to Los Angeles to showcase for key industry players at NBC Universal and industry-wide. Many of the comics from the Best of Stand-Up NBC showcase sign with top Hollywood agents and meet with the entertainment industry's leading casting directors and executives."[56] Second, NBC hosts the NBC Scene Showcase, which is a "6–8 week workshop of original scenes by diverse writers, cast with up-and-coming actors and guided by directors of diverse backgrounds presented in a one-day live theatrical showcase for executives, producers, casting directors, and other industry professionals."[57]

Organizations also provide networking and training opportunities to specific groups of color in the entertainment industry. One such organization is the Coalition of Asian Pacifics in Entertainment (CAPE),[58] an open organization (no membership necessary) that sponsors mixers and workshops on useful subjects, such as professional casting. On its website, CAPE provides professional tips, such as the following for professional actors from a CAPE Casting Workshop at ABC:[59]

1. It's ok to ask for a minute after receiving critique to prep for the next read.
2. Send in postcards to the casting directors. It's a quick and easy way for them to remember you and they have your information on hand.
3. Always remember to keep up the energy, regardless of the genre (comedy v. drama).
4. Always keep the integrity of your resumé—If you haven't done it or don't have that special skill, don't list it!
5. Better to mime than use your own props during an audition.
6. Remember to always read the character breakdown.
7. No matter what you use to display your talent, make sure it's the best work you have before sending it out (e.g., YouTube clips, iPhone videos). Every impression can be a first impression.

The Geena Davis Institute on Gender in Media, founded by Academy Award–winning actor and advocate Geena Davis, is notable as the "only research-based organization working within the media and entertainment industry to engage, educate, and influence the need to dramatically improve, gender balance, reduce stereotyping and create diverse female characters in entertainment targeting children 11 and under."[60] Actors and anyone else interested can purchase a membership and have access to symposiums and salons on gender/racial diversity in the media. One past salon, Reel vs. Real Diversity in Hollywood: Influencers On-Screen and Behind-The Scenes, was hosted by CBS Entertainment in 2014 and featured creators and executive producers of shows such as *Orange Is the New Black* (Netflix), *blackish* (ABC), *Jane the Virgin* (CW), and *Doc*

*McStuffins (*Disney Channel).[61] Actors of color (particularly women) can benefit from such events.

The National Association of Latino Independent Producers (NALIP)[62] is a national membership organization committed to helping Latina/o media makers with their professional goals. It seeks to increase the quality and quantity of stories by and about Latinas/os, through professional development, community building, and mentoring. It has hosted the NALIP media summit for fifteen years; the 2014 keynote speaker and lifetime achievement award winner was Cuban American actor Andy Garcia.

In addition, alternative award shows to the Academy Awards specifically honor artists of color in the entertainment industry. These award shows provide much-needed recognition and publicity to actors of color and other artists of color, who are often overlooked in mainstream award shows, such the 2015 and 2016 Academy Awards. The NAACP hosts the NAACP Image Awards, honoring people of color as actors, actresses, writers, producers, directors, and book authors.[63] The National Council of La Raza (NCLR) hosts the NCLR Alma Awards, recognizing the contributions of Latinas/os in film, television, and music.[64] SAG-AFTRA hosts the American Scene Awards to "honor union productions in the industry that realistically portray the 'American Scene' by intelligently and progressively employing the talents of diverse ethnicities, people with disabilities, women, seniors, people who identify as lesbian, gay, bisexual and/or transgender, and other misrepresented or underrepresented groups."[65]

## Audience Members

While actors of color have a vested interest in seeing greater racial diversity in Hollywood, individual audience members can play an even weightier role by making their voices heard regarding the types of programming they want to see. As the target consumer of a commercial industry, audience members have the power to affect change by demanding more films and television shows with diverse casts. The following are some of the major action points for the average consumer.

### *Watch Diverse Films and Shows*

Put your money where your values are and consume more diverse projects. Buy movie tickets for diverse films and tune into diverse shows on television, streaming video, and web videos. For films, opening weekend box-office sales matter the most to studios and movie theaters, so try to purchase tickets for films with diverse casts on opening weekend. Audiences can also help spread the word about diverse projects through social media and word of mouth. Audiences can find out about diverse projects through independent magazines and websites that focus on pop culture by and/or about people of color and women, such as *Indiewire's Shadow and Act* (http://blogs.indiewire.com/shadowandact/); *Black Girl Nerds* (http://blackgirlnerds.com/); *The Nerds of Color* (https://thenerdsofcolor.org); *The Mary Sue* (http://www.themarysue.com/); and the entertainment/pop culture sections of *Bitch, Colorlines, Ebony, Hyphen, Jet, Latina, Mother Jones*, and *VOXXI*.

### *Boycotts*

Boycotts can pressure broadcast networks to remove stereotypical and offensive programming. One study showed that "the most effective Latino media advocacy campaigns have taken the form of boycotts targeting advertisers in relation to what consumers consider offensive programming or commercials."[66] For the 2016 Academy Awards, both Spike Lee (who won an honorary Oscar in November

2015) and African American actor Jada Pinckett Smith announced their non-attendance of the ceremony. Though they did not organize official boycotts, their announcement quickly elicited a response from the Academy's president, Cheryl Boone Isaacs, who said the Academy planned to take "dramatic steps" to diversify the makeup of its membership.[67] Within four days of Lee's and Smith's announcements, the Academy unanimously decided to implement historic membership changes, including "the appointment of three new governors by the president (typically they are elected by the Academy branches), the diversification of the executive and board committees and new rules that require voting members to be 'active in motion pictures' and to renew that status every 10 years."[68]

Audiences who want to participate in a boycott can organize their own, join other individuals via social media, or align with organizations that monitor media images of particular racial/ethnic groups.

### *The Internet and Social Media*

Letter writing and phone calls are still effective forms of protest, but in Hollywood, social media (particularly Twitter) is gaining momentum as a communication platform for rallying both promotion and protest of films and television shows. One example of using Twitter to promote and support diverse projects comes from the case of *Scandal* (ABC). *Scandal* grew in popularity partly due to live tweets from the show's cast members, particularly star Kerry Washington, and from audience members (many of whom were African American women, the top Twitter user group). One study found that when people, especially cast members and talent, live tweet during a show, more people join in that Twitter conversation.[69] Presumably, more people joining a Twitter conversation means more people are watching the show live—something networks prefer because advertisements are most effective when shows are watched live. Social media is also increasingly driving film box office sales and slumps. The 2015 summer box office saw "wide swings because of immediacy of social media," according to Fox domestic distribution head Chris Aronson.[70] Traditional tracking projections can no longer account for word of mouth on opening night, which is now immediately tweeted out, affecting the successes of films.[71]

Social media is an effective forum to file complaints and instigate protests. Audience members can contact the FCC, the government agency responsible for regulating all forms of communication, through its website (http://www.fcc.gov) and social media (@FCC on Twitter). Audiences can also use social media to protest television networks; film studios; and even individual artists (e.g., directors, executive producers, and actors), many of whom are on social media. Twitter is an especially effective forum for gathering like-minded people for a virtual protest through hashtags. Hashtag activism is the use of a # symbol plus a phrase to unite Twitter users to tweet about a particular issue or policy. For example, #Bringbackourgirls began trending on Twitter as more than one million people, including First Lady Michelle Obama, used the hashtag to tweet their support to retrieve the roughly 250 schoolgirls kidnapped in Nigeria.[72] The biggest hashtag activism to date is #BlackLivesMatter, which developed on Twitter as a response to the killings of unarmed black men and evolved into "the most powerful social justice movement to emerge in the last 50 years."[73]

Hashtag activism has been used to protest racist imagery in Hollywood. Suey Park, a Korean American hashtag activist, used #HowIMetYourRacism to protest the yellowface portrayals on *How I Met Your Mother* (CBS).[74] As a result, one of the co-creators tweeted a public apology. Other hashtag activism against racism in Hollywood has included #EmmaStoned, protesting Emma Stone's playing an Asian character in the film *Aloha* (2015), and #DamonSplaining, calling out Matt Damon's dismissal of Effie Brown's suggestions to cast diverse directors on the television reality show *Project Greenlight* (HBO). Both hashtag protests elicited apologies from the directors.[75] The #OscarsSoWhite hashtag, originally circulated as a critique of the 2015 Oscars, resurfaced for the 2016 Oscars. Because Twitter is heavily monitored by studios and networks due to its ability to make or break a film or show, audience members can use Twitter as a platform for both promotion and protest. At a minimum, apologies by creators and directors indicate their recognition of hashtags; beyond that, hashtags can serve as a form of public accountability and can be paired with other protest measures, such as boycotts.

### *Join an Organization*

Audience members can join organizations that support responsible and proportional representations of people of color in the media. Such organizations monitor racism in the media and organize boycotts and protests, thereby generating greater awareness, affecting change, and getting media coverage. Organizations also provide resources to equip people for media advocacy. In appendix A, I list several major organizations that support artists of color and monitor racism in the media.

Although I recognize that my proposed list of solutions is not exhaustive or even new, I hope these recommended forms of action encourage greater public awareness and engagement. Diversity is not just about the volume of roles, but also about the quality of roles—especially lead roles. We must urge Hollywood to move beyond casting actors of color as background extras and stereotypes, and instead see them as full-range actors capable of embodying a variety of characters. The implications of on-screen diversity go beyond the Hollywood industry, affecting how we feel about ourselves and others. While we are not cultural dupes, mass media can shape our unconscious biases, which in turn can have far-reaching and long-lasting damaging effects on society as a whole.

Industry leaders must take responsibility for Hollywood's diversity problems. White elites should not hide their racial and gender biases behind a facade of colorblind tolerance. Demographic changes and an ever-expanding international box office will put pressure on Hollywood to diversify, but not necessarily to overhaul its longstanding racism. We must transform the industry by taking cues from the actors of color in this book. As African American actor Viola Davis states, "If they exist in life, then we should see it on TV. We should see it on stage or on the screen. As many people are out there are as many stories that should be being told."[76] We must reject the status quo and instead clamor for greater representation of underrepresented groups. We must boycott projects that continue to degrade and exclude actors of color. We must demand and support projects featuring complex protagonists of color. If every reader of this book supports projects featuring actors of color, protests racial exclusion and stereotyping in Hollywood, and joins a media advocacy organization, we can begin a revolution for true racial diversity in Hollywood. Perhaps one day soon, Hollywood will stop showing the false white world of my youth and start representing the United States as it is—full of different stories from folks of every nation and tribe yearning to breathe free.

# APPENDIX A: MEDIA ADVOCACY ORGANIZATIONS

1. Array is an independent film distribution and resource collective comprising arts advocacy organizations, volunteers, and member donors worldwide. Founded by filmmaker Ava DuVernay, Array is, according to its website (http://www.arraynow.com), "dedicated to the amplification of independent films by people of color and women filmmakers globally."
2. Asian Pacific American Media Coalition (APAMC; http://apamediacoalition.wordpress.com) comprises arts and civil rights organizations working on behalf of Asian Americans and Pacific Islanders. It has agreements with ABC, CBS, FOX, and NBC committing these networks to work to increase diversity on-screen and behind the camera. In addition, two of the organizations within APAMC are worth noting for their specific media advocacy work:
   - Asian Americans Advancing Justice (AAJC; http://www.advancingjustice.org) is a civil rights organization working on behalf of Asian Americans and Pacific Islanders (AAPI). It has released research reports on the state of AAPIs in prime-time television as well as report

cards on broadcast television networks (http://www.advancingjustice-aajc.org/news-media/publications/media-diversity-publications-materials).

- Media Action Network for Asian Americans (MANAA; http://manaa.org) is an organization that meets on a monthly basis in Los Angeles to monitor the media and advocate balanced, sensitive, and positive coverage and portrayals of Asian Americans.

3. The Center for Media Justice (http://centerformediajustice.org) is a nationally recognized organizing hub representing the media's policy interests and building the cultural leadership of hundreds of social justice groups across the United States. Its mission is to create media and cultural conditions that strengthen movements for racial justice, economic equity, and human rights.
4. The Geena Davis Institute on Gender in Media (http://seejane.org) is an organization that labors to improve gender balance, reduce stereotyping, and create diverse female characters in entertainment. Its membership is open both to actors and to the general public.
5. The NAACP, particularly the Hollywood chapter (http://beverlyhillshollywoodnaacp.org) has been instrumental in major protests against Hollywood's lack of racial diversity. With its history of protest and research on Hollywood, this is a great organization for any audience member interested in media advocacy and civil rights, particularly with regard (but not limited) to African Americans.
6. National Hispanic Media Coalition (http://www.nhmc.org), which contains the National Latino Media Council, includes the fourteen largest Latina/o civil rights and advocacy organizations in the country. It has a list of campaigns that

audience members can join to advance the representation of Latinas/os in the media. It also releases an annual report card on television.

7. The National Association of Latino Independent Producers (NALIP; http://www.nalip.org) is a national membership organization committed to helping Latina/o media makers with their professional goals. It seeks to increase the quality and quantity of stories by and about Latinas/os through professional development activities, community building, and mentoring.
8. Racebending.com (http://www.racebending.com) is an international grassroots organization of media consumers who support entertainment equality. It advocates for underrepresented groups in entertainment media through protests, boycotts, and advocacy.

# APPENDIX B: METHODS

This book draws upon my dissertation work (original fieldwork and face-to-face interviews), published interviews and published statistics to paint a picture of how actors of color fare in Hollywood. I started my field research on professional actors in 2000, beginning with a pan-ethnic theater group. I branched out from there, continuing my research in various formal and informal theater productions, independent film sets, and professional events with working actors and other industry personnel.

The bulk of my data comes from a hundred face-to-face interviews I conducted with working actors and other Hollywood industry personnel, including writers, casting directors, and talent agents. I interviewed ninety-three working actors within the greater Los Angeles and Hollywood areas. I sampled based on race and gender. My initial sources of sampling ranged from industry personnel I had met through previous research projects to personal networks, followed by snowball sampling to obtain the remaining subjects. I conducted the face-to-face in-depth interviews between 2005 and 2015. The single-session in-person interviews lasted between forty-five minutes and two hours.

I interviewed thirty African American actors, thirty Asian American actors, thirty white actors, and three Latina/o actors. Each group, except Latinas/os, was divided evenly by gender, with fifteen men and fifteen women within each group. I interviewed fewer Latina/o actors because of the time constraints of my dissertation. The actors interviewed ranged from nineteen to sixty-five years old. To supplement these data, I draw on multiple published and broadcast interviews and surveys with Latina/o actors. Besides working actors, I also interviewed other industry experts and personnel. Specifically, I interviewed two heads of diversity at SAG-AFTRA, two talent agents (one was also a manager), a writer, and two casting directors.

To protect the identities of those I interviewed, I used pseudonyms in this book. I used real names only when respondents granted permission or when quoting from publicly accessible secondary sources. Interviews with Hollywood actors enrich existing studies of inequality in the Hollywood industry by providing detailed accounts of how racism, in the form of job exclusion and racial stereotyping, works on the ground.

# NOTES

## INTRODUCTION

1 Tre'vell Anderson, "#Oscarssowhite Creator on Oscar Noms: 'Don't Tell Me That People of Color, Women Cannot Fill Seats,'" *Los Angeles Times,* January 14, 2016, http://www.latimes.com/entertainment/envelope/la-et-mn-april-reign-oscars-so-white-diversity-20160114-story.html.

2 John Horn and Doug Smith, "Diversity Efforts Slow to Change the Face of Oscar Voters," *Los Angeles Times,* December 21, 2013, http://www.latimes.com/entertainment/movies/moviesnow/la-et-mn-diversity-oscar-academy-members-20131221-story.html.

3 David Ng, "Spike Lee and Jada Pinkett Smith to Boycott Oscars; Academy Responds," *Los Angeles Times,* January 18, 2016, http://www.latimes.com/entertainment/movies/la-et-spike-lee-to-boycott-oscars-html-20160118-htmlstory.html.

4 Ben Child, "Oscars 2016: Charlotte Rampling Says Diversity Row Is 'Racist to White People,'" *Guardian,* January 22, 2016, http://www.theguardian.com/film/2016/jan/22/oscars-2016-charlotte-rampling-diversity-row-racist-to-white-people.

5 Yesha Callahan, "#Oscarssowhite: Michael Caine Thinks Blacks Should Be Patient; Charlotte Rampling Says Diversity Complaints Are Racist against Whites," *The Root,* January 22, 2016, http://www.theroot.com/blogs/the_grapevine/2016/01/_oscarssowhite_michael_caine_thinks_blacks_should_be_patient_charlotte_rampling.html.

6 Janice Min, "#OscarsSoWhite: Academy Chiefs Reveal Behind-the-Scenes Drama That Led to Historic Change (Exclusive)," *Hollywood Reporter,* January 27, 2016, http://www.hollywoodreporter.com/features/oscarssowhite-academy-chiefs-reveal-behind-859693.

7 Scott Feinberg, "'Selma' Star David Oyelowo Says Academy Favors 'Subservient' Black Roles," *Hollywood Reporter,* February 2, 2015, http://www.hollywoodreporter.com/race/selma-star-david-oyelowo-says-769032.

8 Ice Cube, *The Angie Martinez Show*, Power 105.1, January 20, 2016, http://www.power1051fm.com/articles/trending-104655/watch-ice-cube-blames-oscar-nomination-14294665.

9 US Population (2014 estimate): US Census, "State and County Quickfacts," http://quickfacts.census.gov/qfd/states/00000.html; lead roles in broadcast television shows (2012–2013) and lead roles in film (2011–2013): Darnell Hunt and Ana-Christina Ramon, "2015 Hollywood Diversity Report: Flipping the Script" (Los Angeles: Ralph J. Bunche Center for African American Studies at UCLA, 2015), 9, 13.

10 I use first name pseudonyms and no surnames for all of my interviewees.

11 After consulting with industry insiders, I use "Hollywood" and "Hollywood industry" to mean the current system of major and minor studios (i.e., majors such as Universal, Disney, and Warner Bros., and minors such as Lionsgate, Summit, and the Weinstein Company), as well as the production companies that are funded and/or distributed in some way by those studios (i.e., Legendary, New Regency, and Amblin). Furthermore, even though funding comes from both international and domestic sources, as long as the primary funding or distribution is funneled through the studios or Hollywood institutions (and not independent sources); the practices of these studios are generalizable to the rest.

12 James E. Short, "How Much Media? 2013 Report on American Consumers," Los Angeles: Institute for Communications Technology Management, Marshall School of Business, University of Southern California, October 2013.

13 Vicky Rideout, "The Common Sense Census: Media Use by Tweens and Teens," San Francisco: Common Sense Media, 2015, 13.

14 Antonio Gramsci, *Selections from Cultural Writings* (Cambridge, MA: Harvard University Press, 1978); James Lull, *Media Communications and Culture: A Global Approach* (New York: Columbia University Press, 1995).

15 Michael Omi, "In Living Color: Race and American Culture," in *Signs of Life in the USA: Readings on Popular Culture for Writers*, ed. S. Maasik and J. Solomon (Boston: Bedford Books, 1997), 500.

16 Max Weisbuch et al., "The Subtle Transmission of Race Bias via Televised Nonverbal Behavior," *Science* 326 (December 18, 2009): 1711.

17 Qingwen Dong and Arthur Phillip Murrillo, "The Impact of Television Viewing on Young Adults' Stereotypes towards Hispanic Americans," *Human Communication* 19, no. 1 (2007); Robert M. Entman and Andrew Rojecki, *The Black Image in the White Mind: Media and Race in America*, Studies in Communication, Media, and Public Opinion (Chicago: University of Chicago Press, 2000).

18 Joe R. Feagin, *Racist America: Roots, Current Realities, and Future Reparations* (New York: Routledge, 2000), 141–142.

19 Jeffrey M. Timberlake et al., "Who 'They' Are Matters: Immigrant Stereotypes and Assessments of the Impact of Immigration," *Social Science Quarterly* 56, no. 2 (2015): 267–299.

20 Sarah Eschholz et al., "Television and Fear of Crime: Program Types, Audience Traits, and the Mediating Effect of Perceived Neighborhood Racial Composition," *Social Problems* 50, no. 3 (2003): 395–415.

21 Ana Swanson, "Whites Greatly Overestimate the Share of Crimes Committed by Black People," *Washington Post*, December 1, 2014, https://www.washingtonpost.com/news/wonk/wp/2014/12/01/whites-greatly-overestimate-the-share-of-crimes-committed-by-black-people.

22 Jamelle Bouie, "Michael Brown Wasn't a Superhuman Demon: But Darren Wilson's Racial Prejudice Told Him Otherwise," *Slate*, November 26, 2014, http://www.slate.com/articles/news_and_politics/politics/2014/11/darren_wilson_s_racial_portrayal_of_michael_brown_as_a_superhuman_demon.single.html; Frederica Boswell, "In Darren Wilson's Testimony, Familiar Themes about Black Men," National Public Radio (November 26, 2014)

23 Donald Bogle, *Toms, Coons, Mulattoes, Mammies, and Bucks: An Interpretive History of Blacks in American Films* (New York: Continuum, 2001), 10.

24 Nazgol Ghandnoosh, "Race and Punishment: Racial Perceptions of Crime and Support for Punitive Policies" (Washington, DC: The Sentencing Project, 2014), http://sentencingproject.org/doc/publications/rd_Race_and_Punishment.pdf.

25 Laura Durkay, "'Homeland' Is the Most Bigoted Show on Television," *Washington Post*, October 2, 2014, https://www.washingtonpost.com/posteverything/wp/2014/10/02/homeland-is-the-most-bigoted-show-on-television.

26 N. Martins and K. Harrison, "Racial and Gender Differences in the Relationship between Children's Television Use and Self-Esteem: A Longitudinal Panel Study," *Communication Research* 39, no. 3 (2011): 338.

27 Michael A. Friedman, "The Harmful Psychological Effects of the Washington Football Mascot," 2013. http://www.changethemascot.org/wp-content/uploads/2013/10/DrFriedmanReport.pdf.

28 "Blackface Minstrelsy," Public Broadcasting System, http://www.pbs.org/wgbh/amex/foster/sfeature/sf_minstrelsy_1.html.

29 Noel Ignatiev, *How the Irish Became White* (New York: Routledge, 1995); David R. Roediger, *The Wages of Whiteness: Race and the Making of the American Working Class*, rev. ed., Haymarket Series. (London: Verso, 1999); Michael Rogin, *Blackface, White Noise: Jewish Immigrants in the Hollywood Melting Pot* (Berkeley: University of California Press, 1996).

30 Robert G. Lee, *Orientals: Asian Americans in Popular Culture* (Philadelphia: Temple University Press, 1999), 34–35.

31 Ibid.

32 Karen Brodkin, *How Jews Became White Folks and What That Says about Race in America* (New Brunswick, NJ: Rutgers University Press, 1998), 156.

33 Stanley Lieberson, *A Piece of the Pie: Blacks and White Immigrants since 1880* (Berkeley: University of California Press, 1980), 32–33.

34 Quoted in Nancy Wang Yuen, "Actors, Asian American," in *Asian American Society: An Encyclopedia*, ed. Mary Yu Danico (Thousand Oaks, CA: Sage, 2014), 18.

35 Feagin, *Racist America;* Lieberson, *A Piece of the Pie;* Michael Omi and Howard Winant, *Racial Formation in the United States: From the 1960s to the 1980s* (New York: Routledge & Kegan Paul, 1986); Mia Tuan, *Forever Foreigners or Honorary Whites?: The Asian Ethnic Experience Today* (New Brunswick, NJ: Rutgers University Press, 1998); Mary C. Waters, *Ethnic Options: Choosing Identities in America* (Berkeley: University of California Press, 1990).

36 Charles Ramírez Berg, *Latino Images in Film: Stereotypes, Subversion, Resistance* (Austin: University of Texas Press, 2002), 68. *Greaser* is a "derogatory American English slang for native Mexicanor Latin American,' first attested 1849, so called from appearance." Definition from *Dictionary.com. Online Etymology Dictionary.* Douglas Harper, Historian. http://www.dictionary.com/browse/greaser.

37 Clint C. Wilson, Félix Gutiérrez, and Lena M. Chao, *Racism, Sexism, and the Media: Multicultural Issues into the New Communications Age,* 4th ed. (Thousand Oaks, CA: Sage, 2013), 77.

38 The Motion Picture Producers and Distributors of America (MPPDA) was the trade association for the major companies in the motion picture industry during the 1920s and 1930s.

39 Laura Serna, "'As a Mexican I Feel It's My Duty:' Citizenship, Cencorship, and the Campaign against Derogatory Films in Mexico, 1922–1930," *The Americas* 63, no. 2 (October 2006): 232.

40 Meredith Simons, "100 Times a White Actor Played Someone Who Wasn't White," *Washington Post,* January 28, 2016, https://www.washingtonpost.com/posteverything/wp/2016/01/28/100-times-a-white-actor-played-someone-who-wasnt-white.

41 Info from http://www.IMDB.com.

42 Susan Courtney, *Hollywood Fantasies of Miscegenation: Spectacular Narratives of Gender and Race, 1903–1967* (Princeton, N.J.: Princeton University Press, 2005), 115–116.

43 Timothy P. Fong, Valerie Soe, and Allan Aquino, "Portrayals in Film and Television," in *Encyclopedia of Asian American Issues Today,* ed. Edith W. Chen and Grace J. Yoo (Westport, CT: Greenwood, 2009): 644.

44 Eithne Quinn, "Closing Doors: Hollywood, Affirmative Action, and the Revitalization of Conservative Racial Politics," *Journal of American History* 99, no. 2 (2012): 466.

45 Ibid., 470.

46 Ibid., 466.

47 American Federation of Television and Radio Artists, "2007–2010 Aftra National Code of Fair Practice for Network Television Broadcasting" (2010).

48 As of 2007, according to Russell Robinson, "Casting and Caste-ing: Reconciling Artistic Freedom and Antidiscrimination Norms," *California Law Review* 95, no. 1 (February 2007): 73.

49 Greg Braxton, "A White, White World on TV's Fall Schedule," *Los Angeles Times,* May 28, 1999, http://articles.latimes.com/1999/may/28/news/mn-41995.

50 Author's analysis of the 2014–2015 prime-time season on broadcast television, based on regular cast listings on the network's own websites, reveals that whites occupied 72 percent of all regular roles, nearly 10 percent above their 2013 US census percentage of 62.6 percent.

51 Motion Picture Association of America, "Theatrical Market Statistics 2014" (Washington, DC: Author, 2015), 12, http://www.mpaa.org/wp-content/uploads/2015/03/MPAA-Theatrical-Market-Statistics-2014.pdf.

52 Stacey Smith, Marc Choueiti, and Katherine Pieper, "Race/Ethnicity in 600 Popular Films: Examining on Screen Portrayals and Behind the Camera Diversity," in *Media, Diversity, and Social Change Initiative* (Los Angeles: University of Southern California Annenberg School for Communication and Journalism, 2014), 1.

53 Simons, "100 Times a White Actor Played Someone Who Wasn't White."

54 Tre'vell Anderson, "Twitter Says a White British Actor Playing a Mexican American Is Exactly What's Wrong with Hollywood," *Los Angeles Times*, January 24, 2016, http://www.latimes.com/entertainment/movies/la-et-mn-charlie-hunnam-edgar-valdez-villarreal-diversity-20160124-story.html; Ben Beaumont-Thomas, "Joseph Fiennes to Play Michael Jackson in 9/11 Road-Trip Drama," *Guardian*, January 26, 2016, http://www.theguardian.com/tv-and-radio/2016/jan/26/joseph-fiennes-michael-jackson-9-11-road-trip-sky-arts.

55 Ryan Gajewski, "Rupert Murdoch Defends 'Exodus' Cast: 'Since When Are Egyptians Not White?'" *Hollywood Reporter*, November 29, 2014, http://www.hollywoodreporter.com/news/rupert-murdoch-defends-exodus-cast-752805.

56 Ruben Navarrette Jr., "Latino Should Have Played Lead in 'Argo,'" *CNN.com* (2013), http://www.cnn.com/2013/01/09/opinion/navarrette-argo-affleck-latino/index.html.

57 Ben Child, "Roger Moore Denies Racist Comments About Idris Elba Playing James Bond," *Guardian*, March 30, 2015, http://www.theguardian.com/film/2015/mar/30/roger-moore-denies-racist-comments-about-idris-elba-playing-james-bond.

58 Eliza Berman, "James Bond Author Apologizes for Calling Idris Elba 'Too Street' to Play 007," *Time*, September 1, 2015, http://time.com/4018556/anthony-horowitz-idris-elba-james-bond.

59 Frances Negron-Muntaner et al., "The Latino Media Gap: A Report on the State of Latinos in U.S. Media" (New York: Center for the Study of Ethnicity and Race, Columbia University, 2014).

60 McKinsey & Company, "Global Media Report 2014: Global Industry Overview" (2014). Plunkett Research, "Introduction to the Sports Industry," Plunkette Research, Ltd., http://www.plunkettresearch.com/sports-recreation-leisure-market-research/industry-trends; David Hunkar, "The World's Five Biggest Alcohol Companies by Market Cap," Seeking Alpha, http://seekingalpha.com/article/198673-the-world-s-five-biggest-alcohol-companies-by-market-cap; American Gaming Association, "State of the States: The Aga Survey of Casino Entertainment" (Washington, DC: Author, 2013).

61 U.S. Department of Labor, "Occupational Employment and Wages—May 2013," in *Bureau of Labor Statistics* (U.S. Department of Labor, 2014).

62 THR Staff, "Hollywood Salaries Revealed, from Movie Stars to Agents (and Even Their Assistants)," *Hollywood Reporter*, October 2, 2014, http://www.hollywoodreporter.com/news/hollywood-salaries-revealed-movie-stars-737321.

63 Jonathan Handel, "Dues for Middle-Class SAG Actors, Most Dual Cardholders Would Decrease in Merger (Analysis)," *Hollywood Reporter*, March 3, 2012, http://www.hollywoodreporter.com/news/sag-aftra-merger-dues-decrease-296663.

64 See appendix B for details on the interview participants and methods.

65 SAG-AFTRA, "Getting Started as an Actor FAQ," SAG-AFTRA, http://www.sagaftra.org/content/getting-started-actor-faq.

66 Erving Goffman, *The Presentation of Self in Everyday Life* (New York: Doubleday Anchor, 1959); Arlie Russell Hochschild, *The Managed Heart: Commercialization of Human Feeling* (Berkeley: University of California Press, 1983); Richard Sennett, *The Fall of Public Man* (New York: Norton, 1974), 107–122.

## CHAPTER 1 HOLLYWOOD'S WHITEST

1 Lanre Bakare, "'Hollywood's Best and Whitest, Sorry . . . Brightest': The Best Oscars 2015 Quotes," *Guardian*, February 23, 2015, http://www.theguardian.com/film/2015/feb/22/oscars-2015-the-best-quotes-of-the-evening.

2 Maane Khatchatourian, "Chris Rock Calls Oscars 'the White People's Choice Awards' in Monologue," *Variety*, February 28, 2016, http://variety.com/2016/film/news/chris-rock-oscars-opening-diversity-race-oscarssowhite-1201717247.

3 US Census, "State and County Quickfacts, USA," 2013. See figure 2 and figure 6 for the percentages of white Hollywood personnel.

4 Russell Robinson, "Casting and Caste-Ing: Reconciling Artistic Freedom and Antidiscrimination Norms," *California Law Review* 95, no. 1 (2007): 7–8.

5 Mary McNamara, "Hollywood to Stop Defining Great Drama as White Men Battling Adversity," *Los Angeles Times*, January 15, 2016, http://www.latimes.com/entertainment/envelope/la-et-st-oscars-mcnamara-notebook-white-hollywood-20160115-column.html.

6 Eithne Quinn, "Closing Doors: Hollywood, Affirmative Action, and the Revitalization of Conservative Racial Politics," *Journal of American History* 99, no. 2 (2012): 471.

7 Directors Guild of America, "Membership," http://www.dga.org/The-Guild/Departments/Membership/Joining-the-DGA.aspx; Producers Guild of America, "Membership Requirements," http://www.producersguild.org/?page=membership_reqs.

8 Public Religion Research Institute, "Analysis | Race and Americans' Social Networks," in *2013 American Values Survey* (Washington, DC: Public Religion Research Institute, 2014), http://publicreligion.org/research/2014/08/analysis-social-network/#.VxDtcBIrLEY.

9 US Commission on Civil Rights, "Window Dressing on the Set: Women and Minorities in Television" (Washington, DC: Author, 1977).

10 Actors of color occupied 28.2 percent of all regular roles, based on my analysis of the 2014–2015 primetime season on broadcast television through coding the regular cast listings on television networks' own websites.

11 Darnell Hunt, Ana-Christina Ramon, and Michael Tran, "2016 Hollywood Diversity Report: Busine$$ as Usual?" (Los Angeles: Ralph J. Bunche Center for African American Studies at UCLA, 2016), 62.

12 Darnell M. Hunt, *Channeling Blackness: Studies on Television and Race in America*, Media and African Americans (New York: Oxford University Press, 2005), 2.

13 Quinn, "Closing Doors," 469.

14 Monica White Ndounou, *Shaping the Future of African American Film: Color-Coded Economics and the Story Behind the Numbers* (New Brunswick, NJ: Rutgers University Press, 2013), 184.

15 This is based on my analysis of the 2014–2015 primetime season on broadcast television based on an examination of regular cast listings on the networks' own websites.

16 Darnell Hunt, "The African American Television Report" (Los Angeles: Screen Actors Guild, 2000).

17 Stacey Smith, Marc Choueiti, and Katherine Pieper, "Race/Ethnicity in 600 Popular Films: Examining on Screen Portrayals and Behind the Camera Diversity," in *Media, Diversity, and Social Change Initiative* (Los Angeles: University of Southern California Annenberg School for Communication and Journalism, 2014), 1.

18 Stacey Smith, Marc Choueiti, and Katherine Pieper, "Media, Diversity, & Social Change Initiative" (Los Angeles: Institute for Diversity and Empowerment at Annenberg, 2016), 8.

19 Ndounou, *Shaping the Future of African American Film.*

20 Rock, "Chris Rock Pens Blistering Essay on Hollywood's Race Problem."

21 Jeannette Walls, "Was Race an Issue in 'Hitch' Casting?," *Today Entertainment* (2005), http://www.today.com/id/7019342/ns/today-entertainment/t/was-race-issue-hitch-casting/#.VpajNpMrLEY.

22 Ibid.

23 Gene Demby, "Remember When You Had to Flip to the Back Page of 'Jet' to Find Black People on TV?," *Codeswitch*, National Public Radio, September 23, 2015, http://www.npr.org/sections/codeswitch/2015/09/23/442191706/remember-when-you-had-to-flip-to-the-back-page-of-jet-to-find-black-people-on-tv.

24 Viola Davis, "Why Viola Davis Says Black Actresses Are in Crisis Mode," in *Oprah's Next Chapter* (Chicago: Harpo Productions, 2013),

http://www.oprah.com/own-oprahs-next-chapter/Why-Viola-Davis-Says-Black-Actresses-Are-in-Crisis-Mode-Video.

25 Smith et al. "Media, Diversity, & Social Change Initiative," 7.

26 Rock, "Chris Rock Pens Blistering Essay on Hollywood's Race Problem."

27 US Census. "State and County Quickfacts, Los Angeles County."

28 Jesse Washington, "Top Hollywood Movies Have Few Roles for Hispanics," Associated Press, August 4, 2014, http://www.cnsnews.com/news/article/few-roles-hispanics-top-hollywood-movies.

29 Frances Negron-Muntaner, Chelsea Abbas, Luis Figueroa, and Samuel Robson, "The Latino Media Gap: A Report on the State of Latinos in U.S. Media" (New York: Center for the Study of Ethnicity and Race, Columbia University 2014), 2.

30 Smith et al. "Media, Diversity, & Social Change Initiative," 8.

31 Lee Hernandez, "Why Gina Rodriguez Is the Golden Globes' Biggest Winner," *Huffington Post* (January 12, 2015), http://www.huffingtonpost.com/lee-hernandez/gina-rodriguez_b_6456964.html.

32 This is based on my analysis of the 2014–2015 prime-time season on broadcast television, coding the regular cast listings on the networks' own websites.

33 Smith et al., "Media, Diversity, & Social Change Initiative," 8.

34 Ana Marie Cox, "Ken Jeong Is Not Cracking Asian Jokes," *New York Times*, December 31, 2015, http://www.nytimes.com/2016/01/03/magazine/ken-jeong-is-not-cracking-asian-jokes.html.

35 Christina Chin et al., "Asian Pacific Americans in Prime Time: Setting the Stage" (Washington, DC: Asian American Justice Center [Now Asian Americans Advancing Justice], 2006); Nancy Wang Yuen et al., "Asian Pacific Americans in Prime Time: Lights, Camera, and Little Action" (Washington DC: National Asian Pacific American Legal Consortium, 2005).

36 Smith et al. "Media, Diversity, & Social Change Initiative," 8.

37 Gavin J. Blair, "'Heroes' Co-Star Masi Oka: 'Hollywood Still Won't Cast Asian Leads,'" *Hollywood Reporter*, March 29, 2013, http://www.hollywoodreporter.com/news/heroes-star-masi-oka-hollywood-431702.

38 Martha M. Lauzen, "It's a Man's (Celluloid) World: On-Screen Representations of Female Characters in the Top 100 Films of 2013" (San Diego: Center for the Study of Women in Television and Film, San Diego State University, 2014).

39 Ibid.

40 Ibid.

41 Tatiana Siegel, "Cannes: Salma Hayek Talks Sexism in Hollywood at 'Women in Motion' Panel," *Hollywood Reporter*, May 16, 2015, http://www.hollywoodreporter.com/news/cannes-2015-salma-hayek-sexism-796121.

42 David Greene and Eric Deggans, "Viola Davis' Emmy Win Shows TV's Power to Shape Perception," in *Morning Edition*, 3:52: National Public Radio, September 21, 2015, http://www.npr.org/2015/09/21/442148912/viola-davis-emmy-win-shows-tvs-power-to-shape-perception.

43 Eric Deggans, Twitter post, September 22, 2015, 2:06 P.M., https://twitter.com/Deggans/status/646430323178389504.

44 Here is the full list of women of color best supporting actress winners: Hattie McDaniel for *Gone With the Wind* in 1939, Miyoshi Umeki for *Sayonara* in 1957, Rita Moreno for *West Side Story* in 1961, Whoopi Goldberg for *Ghost* in 1990, Mercedes Ruehl for *The Fisher King* in 1991, Jennifer Hudson for *Dreamgirls* in 2006, Mo'Nique for *Precious* in 2009, Octavia Spencer for *The Help* in 2011, and Lupita Nyong'o for *12 Years a Slave* in 2013. Academy of Motion Picture Arts and Sciences, "The Official Academy Awards® Database," http://awardsdatabase.oscars.org/ampas_awards/BasicSearchInput.jsp.

45 Jo Piazza, "*Vanity Fair* Takes Heat for Placement of African American Actresses on 'Young Hollywood' Cover," *FoxNews.com*, 2012, www.foxnews.com/entertainment/2012/02/02/vanity-fair-takes-heat-for-placement-african-american-actresses-on-young/.

46 Kyle Buchanan, "Leading Men Age, but Their Love Interests Don't," *Vulture*, April 18, 2013, http://www.vulture.com/2013/04/leading-men-age-but-their-love-interests-dont.html.

47 Melena Ryzik, "What It's Really Like to Work in Hollywood* (*If You're Not a Straight White Man)," *New York Times*, February 24, 2016, http://www.nytimes.com/interactive/2016/02/24/arts/hollywood-diversity-inclusion.html?smid=fb-nytimes&smtyp=cur&_r=0.

48 Robinson, "Casting and Caste-ing," 23.

49 Natalie Robehmed, "The World's Highest-Paid Actors 2015: Robert Downey Jr. Leads with $80 Million Haul," *Forbes*, August 4, 2015, http://www.forbes.com/sites/natalierobehmed/2015/08/04/the-worlds-highest-paid-actors-2015-robert-downey-jr-leads-with-80-million-haul/#1a7c34d42298.

50 Natalie Robehmed, "The World's Highest-Paid Actresses 2015: Jennifer Lawrence Leads with $52 Million," *Forbes*, August 20, 2015, http://www.forbes.com/sites/natalierobehmed/2015/08/20/the-worlds-highest-paid-actresses-2015-jennifer-lawrence-leads-with-52-million/#78ac9d593820.

51 Vanna Le, "Sofia Vergara Is (Once Again) the Highest-Paid TV Actress," *Forbes*, September 3, 2014, http://www.forbes.com/sites/vannale/2014/09/03/sofia-vergara-is-the-highest-paid-tv-actress-of-2014-for-third-year/#5cdcea575673.

52 Rebecca Keegan and Steven Zeitchik, "Oscars 2016: Here's Why the Nominees Are So White—Again," *Los Angeles Times*, January 14, 2016, http://www.latimes.com/entertainment/movies/moviesnow/la-et-mn-all-white-oscar-acting-nominees-20160114-story.html.

53 Michael Pearson, "Matt Damon Apologizes Over 'Project Greenlight' and 'Whitesplaining,'" *CNN.com*, September 17, 2015. http://www.cnn.com/2015/09/17/entertainment/matt-damon-project-greenlight-apology/.

54 Gregg Kilday, "Spike Lee: Getting a Black President Is Easier Than a Black Studio Head," *Hollywood Reporter*, November 14, 2015, http://www.hollywoodreporter.com/news/spike-lee-getting-a-black-840371.

55 Federal Communications Commission, "Report on Ownership of Commercial Broadcast Stations" (Washington, DC: Author 2014): 6–7.

56 Robert Menendez, "Corporate Diversity Report: August 2010," *Senator Robert Menendez*, 2010, http://www.menendez.senate.gov/imo/media/doc/CorporateDiversityReport2.pdf.

57 Meg James and Ben Fritz, "Kevin Tsujihara Is Named Ceo of Warner Bros.," *Los Angeles Times*, January 28, 2013, http://articles.latimes.com/2013/jan/28/business/la-fi-ct-warner-chief-20130129.

58 Mandalit del Barco, "How 'Black Nativity' Made Its Way to the Big Screen," *National Public Radio* (December 5, 2013). http://www.npr.org/blogs/codeswitch/2013/12/06/247504610/how-black-nativity-made-its-way-to-the-big-screen.

59 Ibid.

60 Actor's roundtable on "Intersectional Identities, Labor, and the Entertainment Industry" at the Labor, Entertainment, and Sports Conference on April 18, 2015 at the Crowne Plaza Beverly Hills in Beverly Hills, CA.

61 Directors Guild of America, "Employers Make No Improvement in Diversity Hiring in Episodic Television: DGA Report" (Los Angeles: Author, September 17, 2014), http://www.dga.org/News/PressReleases/2014/140917-Episodic-Director-Diversity-Report.aspx.

62 Directors Guild of America, "DGA TV Diversity Report: Employer Hiring of Women Directors Shows Modest Improvement; Women and Minorities Continue to Be Excluded in First-Time Hiring" (Los Angeles: Author, August 25, 2015), http://www.dga.org/News/PressReleases/2015/150825-Episodic-Director-Diversity-Report.aspx.

63 US Census, "Annual Estimates of the Resident Population by Sex, Age, Race, and Hispanic Origin for the United States and States: April 1, 2010 to July 1, 2012" (Washington, DC:Author, 2013).

64 Lucas Shaw, "Hollywood Dumps Diversity (Again): White Men Directed 90 Percent of This Year's Summer Movies," *The Wrap: Covering Hollywood*, April 7, 2014, http://www.thewrap.com/white-men-directed-90-percent-summer-movies/.

65 Directors Guild of America, "DGA TV Diversity Report."

66 Mark Olsen and Oliver Gettell, "New Facts on Film's 'Epidemic of Invisibility' for Women, Minorities," *Los Angeles Times*, August 6, 2015, http://www.latimes.com/entertainment/movies/la-et-mn-usc-women-movies-20150806-story.html.

67 Stacey Smith and Marc Choueiti, "Black Characters in Popular Film: Is the Key to Diversifying Cinematic Content Held in the Hand of the Black Director?" (Los Angeles: USC Annenberg School for Communication and Journalism, 2011), 3; Stacey Smith, "Whose Work Is Represented by Pop Media?" (Paper presented at the "The Hollywood Shuffle: Exploring Race and Ethnicity Behind and in Front of the Camera," Los Angeles, March 29, 2013).

68 Roger Friedman, "Woody Allen: American Master," *New York Observer*, July 30, 2014, http://observer.com/2014/07/woody-allen-american-master; Lena Dunham, "Lena Dunham Addresses Criticism Aimed at

'Girls,'" on *Fresh Air,* National Public Radio (May 7, 2012), http://www.npr.org/2012/05/07/152183865/lena-dunham-addresses-criticism-aimed-at-girls.

69 Gavin Edwards, "We Shall Overcome: Ava DuVernay on Making 'Selma,'" *Rolling Stone,* January 5, 2015, http://www.rollingstone.com/movies/features/ava-duvernay-on-making-selma-20150105.

70 Quoted in Charles Ramírez Berg, *Latino Images in Film: Stereotypes, Subversion, Resistance* (Austin: University of Texas Press, 2002), 245–246.

71 Jonathan Handel, "Scant Diversity among First-Time TV Directors, Study Finds," *Hollywood Reporter,* September 10, 2015.

72 Al Jean et al., "Writing for Episodic TV: From Freelance to Showrunner" (Los Angeles: Writers Guild of America West, 2004), 41.

73 William T. Bielby and Denise D. Bielby, "'All Hits Are Flukes': Institutionalized Decision Making and the Rhetoric of Network Prime-Time Program Development," *American Journal of Sociology* 99, no. 5 (1994): 1305.

74 Caroline Framke, "Emmys 2015: Viola Davis's Incredible Speech Shows How Far Hollywood Has to Go," *Vox,* September 21, 2015, http://www.vox.com/2015/9/21/9363787/emmys-viola-davis-speech.

75 Greg Braxton, "Panel including Shonda Rhimes address film/TV's 'unconscious bias,'" *Los Angeles Times,* April 21, 2015, http://www.latimes.com/entertainment/tv/showtracker/la-et-st-shonda-rhimes-geena-davis-hollywoods-unconscious-bias-20150420-story.html.

76 Beejoli Shah, "In the White Room with Black Writers: Hollywood's 'Diversity Hires,'" *Defamer,* December 20, 2013, http://defamer.gawker.com/in-the-white-room-with-black-writers-hollywoods-dive-1486789620.

77 Lacey Rose, "'Empire': Meet the Writers behind Broadcast's Biggest Hit," *Hollywood Reporter,* September 17, 2015, http://www.hollywoodreporter.com/live-feed/empire-meet-writers-behind-broadcasts-824097.

78 Rebecca Sun, "TV Diversity Programs: Launching Pad or Scarlet Letter?" *Hollywood Reporter,* October 15, 2015, http://www.hollywoodreporter.com/features/tv-diversity-programs-launching-pad-831880.

79 Aziz Ansari, "Aziz Ansari on Acting, Race, and Hollywood," *New York Times,* November 10, 2015, http://www.nytimes.com/2015/11/15/arts/television/aziz-ansari-on-acting-race-and-hollywood.html.

80 Scott Roxborough, "'Empire' Breaking Barriers with Overseas Viewers," *Hollywood Reporter,* May 6, 2015, http://www.hollywoodreporter.com/news/empire-breaking-barriers-overseas-viewers-792010.

81 Rena Ronson, "'Menage a Trois:' Agents, Talents, Producers" (Paper presented at the "Agents of Change: Talent Agencies in the Transformation of the Film Industry," USC School of Cinematic Arts, Los Angeles, March 7, 2014).

82 Lucy Liu, *East of Main Street: Taking the Lead,* directed by Jonathan Yi (Home Box Office, 2015), DVD.

83 Darnell Hunt and Ana-Christina Ramon, "2015 Hollywood Diversity Report: Flipping the Script" (Los Angeles: Ralph J. Bunche Center for African American Studies at UCLA, 2015), 37–40.

84 Ibid., 39.
85 Ibid., 35–40.
86 Nina Shen Rastogi, "Casting and Race: The Tricky Business of Writing Casting Notices," *Slate.com* (2012), http://www.slate.com/articles/arts/culturebox/2012/07/casting_and_race_the_tricky_business_of_writing_casting_notices.single.html.
87 Harry P. Pachon et al., "Missing in Action: Latinos in and out of Hollywood," ed. Patrick Lee and Joy Hofer (Claremont, CA: The Tomas Rivera Policy Institute, 1999).
88 Laura Barnett, "'Next!': The Secretive World of Casting Directors," *Guardian,* May 21, 2013, http://www.theguardian.com/stage/2013/may/21/casting-directors.
89 Jill Watts, *Hattie McDaniel: Black Ambition, White Hollywood* (New York: Amistad, 2005), 113.
90 Susan Soon He Stanton, "Cast Me If You Can," *Audrey,* Spring 2013, 57.
91 Aasif Mandvi, *East of Main Street: Taking the Lead,* directed by Jonathan Yi (Home Box Office, 2015), DVD.
92 Cameron D. Lippard and Charles A. Gallagher, eds., *Race and Racism in the United States: An Encyclopedia of the American Mosaic* (Westport, CT: Greenwood, 2014), 135.
93 Sut Jhally, "bell hooks: Cultural Criticism and Transformation" (Northampton, MA: Media Education Foundation, 1997).
94 Danielle Cadet, "The 'Straight Outta Compton' Casting Call Is So Offensive It Will Make Your Jaw Drop," *Huffington Post,* July 17, 2014, http://www.huffingtonpost.com/2014/07/17/straight-out-of-compton-casting-call_n_5597010.html.
95 Audie Cornish, "Award-Winning Casting Director Says Diversity Isn't a Trend, It's Evolution," in *Codeswitch* (Washington, DC: National Public Radio, August 25, 2015).
96 W.E.B. Du Bois, *The Souls of Black Folk* (1903). (Mineloa, NY: Dover Publications, 1994), 9.
97 James Lull, "Hegemony," in *Gender, Race, and Class in Media,* ed. Gail Dines and Jean M. Humez (Thousand Oaks, CA: Sage, 2015), 40.
98 Civil Rights Act of 1964, Sec. 2000e-3. [Section 704], http://www.eeoc.gov/laws/statutes/titlevii.cfm.

## CHAPTER 2 HOLLYWOOD'S COLORBLIND RACISM

1 Josh Friedman, "Trio Exits UTA for Endeavor Agency," *Los Angeles Times,* April 7, 2008, http://articles.latimes.com/2008/apr/07/business/fi-agents7.
2 Ibid.
3 Nick Stevens, Q&A session at the "Agents of Change: Talent Agencies in the Transformation of the Film Industry." Los Angeles: University of Southern California School of Cinematic Arts, March 7, 2014.

4 Scott Feinberg, "Academy Members Defend Their Oscar Votes: 'To Imply We Are Racists Is Extremely Offensive,'" *Hollywood Reporter*, January 20, 2016, http://www.hollywoodreporter.com/race/oscars-sowhite-academy-members-defend-oscar-857416.

5 Eduardo Bonilla-Silva, *Racism without Racists: Color-Blind Racism and the Persistence of Racial Inequality in the United States* (Lanham, MD: Rowman & Littlefield, 2006).

6 Scott Feinberg, "Steven Spielberg Supports Diversity in Academy, 'Not 100 Percent Behind' Current Plan, Calls for Limits on Oscar Campaigning (Exclusive)," *Hollywood Reporter*, February 11, 2016, http://www.hollywoodreporter.com/race/steven-spielberg-supports-diversity-academy-864310.

7 Stuart Hall, "Encoding/Decoding," in *Culture, Media, Language*, ed. Stuart Hall et al. (London: Hutchinson, 1980), 128–138.

8 Frank Newport, "Fewer Blacks in U.S. See Bias in Jobs, Income, and Housing," *Gallup Politics* (2013), http://www.gallup.com/poll/163580/fewer-blacks-bias-jobs-income-housing.aspx.

9 Eithne Quinn, "Closing Doors: Hollywood, Affirmative Action, and the Revitalization of Conservative Racial Politics," *Journal of American History* 99, no. 2 (2012): 466–491.

10 Ibid., 475.

11 Russell Robinson, "Casting and Caste-ing: Reconciling Artistic Freedom and Antidiscrimination Norms," *California Law Review* 95, no. 1 (2007): 1–73.

12 Ibid.

13 Joanna Rothkopf, "Watch Viola Davis's Speech as First Woman of Color to Win 'Outstanding Actress' Emmy," *Jezebel*, September 20, 2015. http://jezebel.com/watch-viola-daviss-speech-as-first-woman-of-color-to-wi-1732006898?utm_campaign=socialfow_jezebel_twitter&utm_source=jezebel_twitter&utm_medium=socialflow.

14 Michael Lombardo, "HBO's Michael Lombardo Supports 'Equal Opportunity' Nudity on TV," *The Frame*: KPCC, January 4, 2015, http://www.scpr.org/programs/the-frame/2016/01/04/45792/hbo-s-michael-lombardo-supports-equal-opportunity.

15 Greg Braxton, "NAACP Will Fight Network TV Lineups," *Los Angeles Times*, July 12, 1999, http://articles.latimes.com/1999/jul/12/news/mn-55184.

16 Roger Friedman, "Woody Allen: American Master," *New York Observer*, July 30, 2014, http://observer.com/2014/07/woody-allen-american-master.

17 Sergio, "Woody Allen Says He Won't Hire a Black Actor Unless the Role Calls for One . . . Whatever That Means," *Shadow and Act: On Cinema of the African Diaspora* (July 31, 2014), http://blogs.indiewire.com/shadowandact/woody-allen-says-he-wont-hire-a-black-actor-unless-the-role-calls-for-one-20140731.

18 Arienne Thompson, "When It Comes to Diversity, Hollywood's Lost in the 'Woods,'" *USA Today*, January 9, 2015, http://www.usatoday.com/

story/life/movies/2015/01/09/hollywood-lacks-diversity-into-the-woods-exodus/20693591.

19 Pam Lambert, "What's Wrong with This Picture? Exclusion of Minorities Has Become a Way of Life in Hollywood," *People* 45, no. 11 (March 18, 1996), http://www.people.com/people/archive/article/0,,20103043,00.html.

20 Sadie Gennis, "Kenan Thompson Blames SNL's Diversity Issue on Lack of Talented Black Comediennes," *TVGuide.com* (2013), http://www.tvguide.com/news/snl-diversity-issue-kenan-thompson-1072056.aspx.

21 Wayman Wong, "Actors Remember Pacific Overtures," *Sondheim Review* 4, no. 4 (Spring 1998), https://www.sondheimreview.com/magazine/vol-4-no-4-spring-1998/.

22 Quinn, "Closing Doors," 483. For a contemporary article from the time critiquing Black Exploitation films, see Henry W. McGee III, "Black Movies: A New Wave of Exploitation." *Harvard Crimson* (1972), http://www.thecrimson.com/article/1972/10/10/black-movies-a-new-wave-of/?page=single.

23 Quinn, "Closing Doors," 484.

24 Ibid., 483.

25 Nellie Andreeva, "Pilots 2015: The Year of Ethnic Castings," *Deadline Hollywood*, March 24, 2015, http://deadline.com/2015/03/tv-pilots-ethnic-casting-trend-backlash-1201386511.

26 Charles McNulty, "Broadway Musical 'Hamilton' Could Teach Oscar a Lesson on Diversity," *Los Angeles Times*, January 28, 2016, http://www.latimes.com/entertainment/arts/la-et-cm-hamilton-notebook-20160128-column.html.

27 Robinson, "Casting and Caste-ing," 73.

28 Gloria Goodale, "What's Missing from This Picture?," *Christian Science Monitor*, August 6, 1999, http://www.csmonitor.com/1999/0806/p13s1.html.

29 US Census, "New York (City), New York" (2010).

30 Lena Dunham, "Lena Dunham Addresses Criticism Aimed at 'Girls,'" *Fresh Air*, National Public Radio, May 7, 2012, http://www.npr.org/2012/05/07/152183865/lena-dunham-addresses-criticism-aimed-at-girls.

31 Eliana Dockterman, "Sofia Vergara on Taking Risks as an Actor: 'It's Not Like We're Doing Brain Surgery,'" *Time*, October 22, 2014, http://time.com/3531603/sofia-vergara-interview-thyroid-cancer.

32 Christopher Nolan, "Christopher Nolan: Interstellar," *The Treatment*, KCRW, November 12, 2014, http://www.kcrw.com/news-culture/shows/the-treatment/christopher-nolan-interstellar.

33 Scott Cooper, "Scott Cooper: Out of the Furnace," *The Treatment*, KCRW, December 18, 2013, http://www.kcrw.com/news-culture/shows/the-treatment/scott-cooper-out-of-the-furnace.

34 Danny Strong, "'Empire's' Danny Strong on Writing outside His Comfort Zone," *The Business*, KCRW, March 23, 2015, http://www.kcrw.com/news-culture/shows/the-business/empires-danny-strong-on-writing-outside-his-comfort-zone.

35 Debra Birnbaum, "Viola Davis on Her Groundbreaking Emmy Win: 'I Felt Like I Fulfilled a Purpose,'" *Variety*, September 23, 2015, http://variety.com/2015/tv/news/viola-davis-emmy-how-to-get-away-with-murder-1201600239.

36 Adam Moore, phone interview by author, digital recording, Los Angeles, December 12, 2012.

37 Allison Samuels and John Leland, "They've Got Next," *Newsweek*, April 5, 1999, http://www.newsweek.com/theyve-got-next-164784. Though Keith David played Cameron Diaz's character's stepfather, the role is relatively small and the film centers around the white character's lives.

38 Robinson, "Casting and Caste-ing," 8.

39 Tory Metzger, "'Menage a Trois': Agents, Talents, Producers." Paper presented at the "Agents of Change: Talent Agencies in the Transformation of the Film Industry." Los Angeles: University of Southern California School of Cinematic Arts, March 7, 2014.

40 Scott Foundas, "'Exodus: Gods and Kings' Director Ridley Scott on Creating His Vision of Moses," *Variety*, November 25, 2014, http://variety.com/2014/film/news/ridley-scott-exodus-gods-and-kings-christian-bale-1201363668.

41 Robinson, "Casting and Caste-ing," 58.

42 Chon A. Noriega, "The Numbers Game," *Jump Cut: A Review of Contemporary Media* 39 (1994), http://www.ejumpcut.org/archive/onlinessays/JC39folder/numbersGame.html.

43 Melissa Silverstein, "Women Are the Successes of the Summer Box Office," *Forbes*, September 5, 2014, http://www.forbes.com/sites/melissasilverstein/2014/09/05/women-are-the-successes-of-the-summer-box-office/#12a3afab1ea1.

44 Harry P. Pachon et al., "Missing in Action: Latinos in and out of Hollywood," ed. Patrick Lee and Joy Hofer (Claremont, CA: Tomas Rivera Policy Institute, 1999).

45 Monica White Ndounou, *Shaping the Future of African American Film: Color-Coded Economics and the Story Behind the Numbers* (New Brunswick, NJ: Rutgers University Press, 2013), 183.

46 Russell Robinson, "Hollywood's Race/Ethnicity and Gender-Based Casting: Prospects for a Title VII Lawsuit," in *Latino Policy and Issues Brief*, ed. Chon Noriega (Los Angeles: University of California, 2006), 4.

47 Ibid.

48 Andrew J. Weaver, "The Role of Actors' Race in White Audiences' Selective Exposure to Movies," *Journal of Communication* 61 (2011): 378.

49 Ibid.

50 Linda Ge, "How ABC Is Trailblazing Path for Asians on TV with 'Fresh Off the Boat,' 'Dr. Ken,' 'Quantico,'" *The Wrap: Covering Hollywood*, September 26, 2015, http://www.thewrap.com/how-abc-is-trailblazing-path-for-asians-on-tv-with-fresh-off-the-boat-dr-ken-quantico/.

51 Pew Research Center, "Millennials in Adulthood: Detached from Institutions, Networked with Friends," *Pew Research Social & Demographic Trends* (2014), http://www.pewsocialtrends.org/2014/03/07/millennials-in-adulthood/.

52 Hope Yen, "Census: White Population Will Lose Majority in U.S. by 2043," *Huffington Post*, December 12, 2012, http://www.huffingtonpost.com/2012/12/12/census-hispanics-and-black-unseat-whites-as-majority-in-united-states-population_n_2286105.html.

53 US Census, "State and County Quickfacts: Peoria County, Illinois" (2013).

54 Motion Picture Association of America, "Theatrical Market Statistics 2014" (Washington, DC: Author, 2015), 12.

55 Nielsen, "Multifaceted Connections: African-American Media Usage Outpaces across Platforms," *Newswire*, February 3, 2015, http://www.nielsen.com/us/en/insights/news/2015/multifaceted-connections-african-american-media-usage-outpaces-across-platforms.html.

56 Motion Picture Association of America, "Theatrical Market Statistics 2014," 13.

57 Nielsen, "State of the Asian American Consumer: Growing Market, Growing Impact" (New York: Author, 2012), 10. Nielsen, "Asian Americans: Culturally Connected and Forging the Future" (New York: Author, 2015), 25.

58 Darnell Hunt and Ana-Christina Ramon, "2015 Hollywood Diversity Report: Flipping the Script" (Los Angeles: Ralph J. Bunche Center for African American Studies at UCLA, 2015).

59 Amy Kaufman, "On Biggest Memorial Day Ever, 'Fast & Furious 6' Laps 'Hangover III,'" *Los Angeles Times*, May 27, 2013, http://articles.latimes.com/2013/may/27/entertainment/la-et-ct-box-office-fast-furious-hangover-part-3-20130527. Previously, Latinos also made up 46 percent of the *Fast & Furious 4* audience, demonstrating the purchasing power of people of color. Reed Johnson, "Fast & Furious' Taps into Latino Market," *Los Angeles Times*, April 7, 2009, http://articles.latimes.com/2009/apr/07/entertainment/et-carlatino7.

60 Jonathon Dornbush, "Furious 7 Races Past $1 Billion Mark at Worldwide Box Office in Record Time," *Entertainment Weekly*, April 17, 2015, http://www.ew.com/article/2015/04/17/furious-7–1-billion-box-office.

61 Jordi McKenzie, "Do 'African American' Films Perform Better or Worse at the Box Office? An Empirical Analysis of Motion Picture Revenues and Profits," *Applied Economics Letters* 17, no. 16 (2010): 1559–1564.

62 Ndounou, *Shaping the Future of African American Film*, 3.

63 Taryn Finley, "Films with Leading Black Actors Land Top Spot at the Box Office for Five Consecutive Weeks," *Huffington Post*, September 14, 2015, http://www.huffingtonpost.com/entry/films-with-black-actors-land-top-spot-at-the-box-office-for-5-consecutive-weeks_55f6dec7e4b063ecbfa4d8b0.

64 Ben Fritz and John Horn, "Reel China: Hollywood Tries to Stay on China's Good Side," *Los Angeles Times*, March 16, 2011, http://articles.latimes.com/2011/mar/16/entertainment/la-et-china-red-dawn-20110316; Paul Bond, "DreamWorks Animation to Launch TV Channel in Asia," *Hollywood Reporter*, December 9, 2014, http://www.hollywoodreporter.com/news/dreamworks-animation-launch-tv-channel-755631.

65 Anousha Sakoui, "China Could Beat Hollywood by 2017," *Bloomberg News*, February 24, 2016, http://www.bloomberg.com/news/articles/2016-02-25/china-could-beat-hollywood-by-2017.

66 Neda Ulaby, "Hollywood's New Strategy: Supporting Chinese-Made Blockbusters," *Codeswitch*, National Public Radio, November 25, 2013.

67 Frank Pallotta and Brian Stelter, "African-Americans Propel Prime Time TV Hits Like 'Empire,'" *CNN.com*, January 28, 2015, http://money.cnn.com/2015/01/28/media/empire-blackish-murder/.

68 Kevin Fallon, "#Oscarssowhite: How a Lack of Diversity Historically Dooms Oscars Ratings," *Daily Beast*, January 26, 2016, http://www.thedailybeast.com/articles/2016/01/27/oscarssowhite-how-a-lack-of-diversity-historically-dooms-oscars-ratings.html.

69 Scott Williams, "ABC's 'All American Girl' Leads New Series in Ratings Victory," Associated Press, September 20, 1994, http://www.apnewsarchive.com/1994/ABC-s-All-American-Girl-Leads-New-Series-in-Ratings-Victory/id-a51b1e3807bd34a13acf86e32b7ba7fa.

70 E-Media Programming, "Sunny vs Seinfeld: A Tale of Ratings," May 6, 2011, http://brbsprogramming.wordpress.com/2011/05/06/sunny-vs-seinfeld-a-tale-of-ratings/.

71 Glenn Whipp, "Aiming to Diversify Storytelling, Ava Duvernay Expands Scope of Film Distribution Collective," *Los Angeles Times*, September 8, 2015, http://www.latimes.com/entertainment/movies/la-et-mn-ava-duvernay-20150908-story.html.

72 Ibid.

73 Marlow Stern, "Octavia Spencer on Hollywood and Race: The Film Roles I'm Offered Are Too Small," *Daily Beast*, July 31, 2014, http://www.thedailybeast.com/articles/2014/07/31/octavia-spencer-on-hollywood-and-race-the-film-roles-i-m-offered-are-too-small.html.

74 Ndounou, *Shaping the Future of African American Film*, 1.

75 Elodie Bardinet, "Creed Devient le 20e Film Millionnaire de Sylvester Stallone en France," *Premiere*, January 26, 2016, http://www.premiere.fr/Cinema/News-Cinema/Creed-devient-le-20e-film-millionnaire-de-Sylvester-Stallone-en-France.

76 Scott Roxborough, "'Empire' Breaking Barriers with Overseas Viewers," *Hollywood Reporter*, May 6, 2015, http://www.hollywoodreporter.com/news/empire-breaking-barriers-overseas-viewers-792010.

77 Ndounou, *Shaping the Future of African American Film*, 231–232.

78 Robert M. Entman, and Andrew Rojecki, *The Black Image in the White Mind: Media and Race in America*, Studies in Communication, Media, and Public Opinion (Chicago: University of Chicago Press, 2000), 72.

79 Mannie Holmes, "ABC Apologizes for Confusing 'Quantico's' Priyanka Chopra with Another Indian Actress," *Variety*, September 29, 2015, http://variety.com/2015/tv/news/abc-priyanka-chopra-apology-quantico-1201605597/.

80 Dominic Patten, "Golden Globes Embarrassingly Confuse Gina Rodriguez with America Ferrera," *Deadline Hollywood*, December 10, 2015,

http://deadline.com/2015/12/golden-globes-america-ferrera-gina-rodriguez-confusion-jane-the-virgin-1201664471/.

81 Alan Yang, Twitter post, January 19, 2016, 10:54 A.M., https://twitter.com/AlanMYang/status/689521402261676033.

82 Roberto A. Ferdman, "How Americans Pretend to Love 'Ethnic Food,'" *Washington Post*, April 22, 2016, https://www.washingtonpost.com/news/wonk/wp/2016/04/22/the-great-ethnic-food-lie/?tid=sm_fb.

83 Joann Faung Jean Lee, *Asian American Actors: Oral Histories from Stage, Screen, and Television* (Jefferson, NC: McFarland, 2000), 114.

## CHAPTER 3 HOLLYWOOD'S TYPECASTING

1 E. W. Zuckerman et al., "Robust Identities or Nonentities? Typecasting in the Feature-Film Labor Market," *American Journal of Sociology* 108, no. 5 (2003): 1021.

2 Jason Serafino, "The 10 Most Typecast Actors of All Time," *Complex*, November 26, 2012, http://www.complex.com/pop-culture/2012/11/10-most-typecast-actors-of-all-time/.

3 Donald Bogle, *Toms, Coons, Mulattoes, Mammies, and Bucks: An Interpretive History of Blacks in American Films* (New York: Continuum, 2001), 241.

4 Alex Wong, "Fresh Off the Boat's Constance Wu Still Isn't Sure About This Whole TV Thing," *Gentleman's Quarterly*, September 21, 2015, http://www.gq.com/story/fresh-off-the-boat-constance-wu-isnt-sure-whole-tv-thing.

5 Richard D. Alba, *Ethnic Identity: The Transformation of White America* (New Haven: Yale University Press, 1990); Karen Brodkin, *How Jews Became White Folks and What That Says about Race in America* (New Brunswick, NJ: Rutgers University Press, 1998); Joe R. Feagin, *Racist America: Roots, Current Realities, and Future Reparations* (New York: Routledge, 2000); Noel Ignatiev, *How the Irish Became White* (New York: Routledge, 1995); Charles Jaret and Donald C. Reitzes, "The Importance of Racial-Ethnic Identity and Social Setting for Blacks, Whites, and Multiracials," *Sociological Perspectives* 42, no. 4 (Winter, 1999), 711–737; Stanley Lieberson, *A Piece of the Pie: Blacks and White Immigrants since 1880* (Berkeley: University of California Press, 1980); Mary C. Waters, *Ethnic Options: Choosing Identities in America* (Berkeley: University of California Press, 1990).

6 Gail Sullivan, "John Cho of 'Selfie': 'I Experienced Racism,'" *Washington Post*, October 9, 2014, https://www.washingtonpost.com/news/morning-mix/wp/2014/10/09/john-cho-of-selfie-wants-roles-outside-any-asian-stereotype-2/.

7 Kristin Anderson, "Character Counts," *Vanity Fair*, March 2012, http://www.vanityfair.com/hollywood/2012/03/hollywoods-best-character-actors.

8 Ibid.

9 Raymond Wong, "To Avoid or to Embrace? How Actors Navigate Stereotypes," in *Talk of the Nation*, National Public Radio, May 1, 2013.

10 Jarett Wieselman, "The Woman Leading a Crusade to Tell More Asian-American Stories," *BuzzFeed News*, September 17, 2015. http://www.buzzfeed.com/jarettwieselman/constance-wu-crusade-to-be-seen-as-more-than-a-sidekick?utm_term=.ugoKVo3XYe—.kjPm5GRdL.

11 Harry P. Pachon et al., "Missing in Action: Latinos in and out of Hollywood," ed. Patrick Lee and Joy Hofer (Claremont, CA: The Tomas Rivera Policy Institute, 1999).

12 Frances Negron-Muntaner, Chelsea Abbas, Luis Figueroa, and Samuel Robson, "The Latino Media Gap: A Report on the State of Latinos in U.S. Media" (New York: Center for the Study of Ethnicity and Race, Columbia University 2014), 19.

13 Vincent Schilling, "Native Actors Walk Off Set of Adam Sandler Movie after Insults to Women, Elders," *Indian Country Today Media Network.com* (2015), http://indiancountrytodaymedianetwork.com/2015/04/23/native-actors-walk-set-adam-sandler-movie-after-insults-women-elders-160110.

14 Bryan Llenas, "Tip of the Hat to Legend Rita Moreno: Lifetime Achievement Award Winner, with Puerto Rico in Mind," *Fox News Latino* (2014), http://latino.foxnews.com/latino/entertainment/2014/01/17/sag-awards-2014-living-legend-rita-moreno-will-receive-biggest-award-with/.

15 Monica White Ndounou, *Shaping the Future of African American Film: Color-Coded Economics and the Story Behind the Numbers* (New Brunswick, NJ: Rutgers University Press, 2013), 16–17.

16 Patricia Reynoso, "Gina Rodriguez on *Jane the Virgin*, Her Outspoken Attitude, and Embracing Her Natural Beauty," *Glam Belleza Latina*, June 9, 2015, http://www.glamour.com/story/newbie-actress-gina-rodriguez.

17 Quoted in Jill Watts, *Hattie McDaniel: Black Ambition, White Hollywood* (New York: Amistad, 2005), 136.

18 Amanda Terkel, "Lisa Chan, Actress in Pete Hoekstra China Ad, Apologizes: 'It Was Absolutely a Mistake,'" *Huffington Post* (2012), http://www.huffingtonpost.com/2012/02/15/lisa-chan-pete-hoekstra-apologizes_n_1280271.html.

19 Ibid.

20 Suzy Nakamura, "Dr. Ken: Sneak Preview" (presentation, Japanese American National Museum, Los Angeles, CA, September 24, 2015).

21 Ken Jeong, "Dr. Ken: Sneak Preview" (presentation, Japanese American National Museum, Los Angeles, CA, September 24, 2015).

22 Michael O'Connell, "'How I Met Your Mother' Creators Respond to Kung Fu Controversy," *Hollywood Reporter*, January 15, 2014, http://www.hollywoodreporter.com/live-feed/how-i-met-your-mother-671349.

23 Sidney Poitier, "Oprah Talks to Sidney Poitier," *O*, October 2000, http://www.oprah.com/omagazine/Oprah-Interviews-Sidney-Poitier.

24 Rebecca Ford, "'Birth of a Nation': The Slave-Revolt Movie That Will Have Sundance Talking," *Hollywood Reporter*, January 20, 2016,

http://www.hollywoodreporter.com/features/birth-a-nation-slave-revolt-857177.

25 *Latinos Beyond Reel: Challenging a Media Stereotype,* directed by Miguel Picker and Chyng Sun (2012; Northampton, MA: Media Education Foundation), DVD.

26 Randall Park, "What It Means to Star on Network TV's First Asian American Family Sitcom in 20 Years," *KoreAm*, June 3, 2014, http://iamkoream.com/what-it-means-to-be-on-network-tvs-first-asian-american-family-sitcom-in-20-years/.

## CHAPTER 4 HOLLYWOOD'S DOUBLE BIND

1 Thierry Devos and Mahzarin R. Banaji, "American = White?" *Journal of Personality and Social Psychology.* 88, no. 3 (March 2005): 447–466.

2 Tiffany Bakker, "True Colors," *Net-a-Porter,* May 9, 2013, http://www.tiffanybakker.com/wp-content/uploads/2014/10/Lucy-liu.pdf.

3 Thierry Devos and Debbie S. Ma, "Is Kate Winslet More American Than Lucy Liu? The Impact of Construal Processes on the Implicit Ascription of a National Identity," *British Psychological Society* 47 (2008): 191–215.

4 John Cho, "John Cho Reflects on His Career," Center for Asian American Media, September 22, 2014, http://caamedia.org/blog/2014/09/22/john-cho-reflects-on-his-career/.

5 Carolina Moreno, "Revelations from the Stars of 'Orange Is the New Black,'" *Huffington Post,* June 6, 2014, http://www.huffingtonpost.com/2014/06/06/orange-is-the-new-black-latinas_n_5462209.html.

6 Lupe Ontiveros, "Latina Actress Aims to Break Maid Stereotype," *All Things Considered*, National Public Radio, April 12, 2009.

7 Jun Xing, *Asian America through the Lens: History, Representations, and Identity* (Walnut Creek, CA: AltaMira Press, 1998), 67.

8 Harry P. Pachon et al., "Missing in Action: Latinos in and out of Hollywood," ed. Patrick Lee and Joy Hofer (Claremont, CA: The Tomas Rivera Policy Institute, 1999).

9 Anna Brown, "U.S. Hispanic and Asian Populations Growing, but for Different Reasons," *Factank: News in the Numbers,* June 26, 2014, http://www.pewresearch.org/fact-tank/2014/06/26/u-s-hispanic-and-asian-populations-growing-but-for-different-reasons/.

10 "Latino Americans: Timeline of Important Dates," Washington Educational Television Association (WETA). Washington, DC, Bosch and Co., Inc., Latino Public Broadcasting, September 12, 2013, http://www.pbs.org/latino-americans/en/timeline/.

11 Loni Ding, "Ancestors in the Americas: Asian American Timeline," National Asian American Telecommunications Association, March 30, 2001, http://www.pbs.org/ancestorsintheamericas/timeline.html.

12 Rita Moreno, "Rita Moreno Acts Out Own Career in 'Life without Makeup,'" Public Broadcasting Sstyem, KQED. San Francisco, September 30, 2011.

13 Pachon et al., "Missing in Action."
14 Ibid.
15 Gabriel Lerman, "Oscar Isaac and His Secret Weapon," *IN: The In-Flight Magazine of LAN* (Línea Aérea Nacional), 2014.
16 Debra Bell, "10 Things You Didn't Know about Kal Penn," *U.S. News & World Report*, April 8, 2009, http://www.usnews.com/news/obama/articles/2009/04/08/10-things-you-didnt-know-about-kal-penn; Tony Wong, "Actress Chloe Bennet Says Changing Her Name Changed Her Luck," *Star*, May 11, 2014, http://www.thestar.com/entertainment/television/2014/05/11/actress_chloe_bennet_says_changing_her_name_changed_her_luck.html.
17 Sara Loscos, "Having an Accent in America: An Actor Speaks," in *The World*, Public Radio International (September 18, 2013).
18 *Latin Gossip Staff, "Roselyn Sanchez Talks about Her Accent Debacle," Latin Gossip (2010),* http://www.latingossip.com/roselyn-sanchez/roselyn-sanchez-talks-about-her-accent-debacle.htm*l*.
19 Loscos, "Having an Accent in America."
20 E. Alex Jung, "*All-American Girl* at 20: The Evolution of Asian Americans on TV," *Los Angeles Review of Books*, November 9, 2014, http://lareviewofbooks.org/article/american-girl-20-evolution-asian-americans-tv.
21 Pachon et al., "Missing in Action."
22 Melena Ryzik, "What It's Really Like to Work in Hollywood* (*If You're Not a Straight White Man)," *New York Times*, February 24, 2016, http://www.nytimes.com/interactive/2016/02/24/arts/hollywood-diversity-inclusion.html?smid=fb-nytimes&smtyp=cur&_r=0.
23 mun2, "Black and Latino, Digital Film," Telemundo Digital Network, January 11, 2012, http://www.mun2.tv/candy/original/black-and-latino; Pachon et al., "Missing in Action."
24 Pachon et al., "Missing in Action."
25 Ibid.
26 Ryzik, "What It's Really Like to Work in Hollywood.
27 Liz Mundy, "Cracking the Bamboo Ceiling." *Atlantic*, October 14, 2014, http://www.theatlantic.com/magazine/archive/2014/11/cracking-the-bamboo-ceiling/380800/.

## CHAPTER 5 SURVIVING HOLLYWOOD

1 Priska Neely, "To Avoid or to Embrace? How Actors Navigate Stereotypes," *Talk of the Nation*, National Public Radio, May 1, 2013.
2 Marlon T. Riggs et al., *Color Adjustment* (San Francisco, CA: California Newsreel, 1991).
3 Nina Bandelj, "How Method Actors Create Character Roles," *Sociological Forum* 18, no. 3 (2003): 392; "What Is Method Acting," *Lee Strasberg Theatre and Film Institute*, http://newyork.methodactingstrasberg.com/what-is-method-acting/.

4 Arlie Russell Hochschild, *The Managed Heart: Commercialization of Human Feeling* (Berkeley: University of California Press, 1983).
5 A. G. Murphy, "The Dialectical Gaze—Exploring the Subject-Object Tension in the Performances of Women Who Strip," *Journal of Contemporary Ethnography* 32, no. 3 (2003): 329.
6 Helena Andrews, "Here's Why Retta Should MC Every Washington Gala Ever," *Washington Post,* March 20, 2015, https://www.washingtonpost.com/news/reliable-source/wp/2015/03/20/heres-why-retta-should-mc-every-washington-gala-ever/.
7 Neely, "To Avoid or to Embrace?"
8 Shirley Jennifer Lim, *A Feeling of Belonging: Asian American Women's Public Culture, 1930–1960,* American History and Culture (New York: New York University Press, 2006), 58.
9 Monica White Ndounou, *Shaping the Future of African American Film: Color-Coded Economics and the Story Behind the Numbers* (New Brunswick, NJ: Rutgers University Press, 2013), 210.
10 Neely, "To Avoid or to Embrace?"
11 Quoted in Jill Watts, *Hattie McDaniel: Black Ambition, White Hollywood* (New York: Amistad, 2005), 139.
12 Tanzina Vega, "An Emerging Hispanic Voice Defends Her 'Maids,'" *New York Times,* June 24, 2013, http://www.nytimes.com/2013/06/25/business/media/an-emerging-hispanic-voice-defends-her-maids.html.
13 Neely, "To Avoid or to Embrace?"
14 Quoted in Emilie Raymond, *Stars for Freedom: Hollywood, Black Celebrities, and the Civil Rights Movement* (Seattle: University of Washington Press, 2015), 23–24.
15 Quoted in Susan Soon He Stanton, "Cast Me If You Can," *Audrey* (2013), 57.
16 Nancy Wang Yuen, "Playing 'Ghetto': Black Actors, Stereotypes, and Authenticity," in *Black Los Angeles: American Dreams and Racial Realities,* ed. Darnell Hunt and Ana-Christina Ramon (New York: New York University Press, 2010), 237.
17 Ada Tseng, "Audrey Fall 2015 Cover Story: Constance Wu," *Audrey,* August 27, 2015, http://audreymagazine.com/audrey-fall-2015-cover-story-constance-wu/.
18 Sofia Vergara, "Sofia Vergara: I Don't Worry about Latin Stereotypes 'At All,'" *Huffpost Live,* June 4, 2013, http://live.huffingtonpost.com/r/highlight/51ae2dc078c90a5bfe0000a5.
19 Yuen, "Playing 'Ghetto,'" 236.
20 *East of Main Street: Taking the Lead,* directed by Jonathan Yi (Home Box Office, 2015), DVD.
21 Neely, "To Avoid or to Embrace?"

## CHAPTER 6 CHALLENGING HOLLYWOOD

1 Melena Ryzik, "What It's Really Like to Work in Hollywood* (*If You're Not a Straight White Man)," *New York Times,* February 24, 2016, http://www.nytimes.com/interactive/2016/02/24/arts/hollywood-diversity-inclusion.html?smid=fb-nytimes&smtyp=cur&_r=0.

2 Stuart Hall, "Culture, Media, and the 'Ideological Effect,'" in *Mass Communication and Society,* ed. J. Curran, M. Gurevitch, and J. Woollacott (London: Edward Arnold, 1977), 333.
3 "Gilbert Roland Wears Famous Old Costumes," *Citizen,* January 7, 1928.
4 Charles Ramírez Berg, *Latino Images in Film: Stereotypes, Subversion, Resistance* (Austin: University of Texas Press, 2002), 98–100.
5 Jill Watts, *Hattie McDaniel: Black Ambition, White Hollywood* (New York: Amistad, 2005), 164.
6 Quoted in Emilie Raymond. *Stars for Freedom: Hollywood, Black Celebrities, and the Civil Rights Movement* (Seattle: University of Washington Press, 2015), 31.
7 Eliana Dockterman, "Sofia Vergara on Taking Risks as an Actor: 'It's Not Like We're Doing Brain Surgery,'" *Time,* October 22, 2014, http://time.com/3531603/sofia-vergara-interview-thyroid-cancer/.
8 Vincent Schilling, "Native Actors Walk Off Set of Adam Sandler Movie after Insults to Women, Elders," *Indian Country Today Media Network.com,* April 23, 2015, http://indiancountrytodaymedianetwork.com/2015/04/23/native-actors-walk-set-adam-sandler-movie-after-insults-women-elders-160110.
9 Ibid.
10 Stephanie Beatriz, "Stephanie Beatriz Talks "Brooklyn Nine-Nine" and Being Latina W/ Robert Herrera," *Frontrowlive.ent.,* https://www.youtube.com/watch?v=REicqqqbC-c#t=149.
11 Nancy Wang Yuen, "Performing Race, Negotiating Identity: Asian American Professional Actors in Hollywood," in *Asian American Youth Culture, Identity, and Ethnicity,* ed. Jennifer Lee and Min Zhou (New York: Routledge, 2004), 260.
12 Quoted in Raymond, *Stars for Freedom,* 28.
13 Nancy Wang Yuen, "Playing 'Ghetto': Black Actors, Stereotypes, and Authenticity," in *Black Los Angeles: American Dreams and Racial Realities,* ed. Darnell Hunt and Ana-Christina Ramon (New York: New York University Press, 2010), 239.
14 Yvette Nicole Brown, "'Community': Alison Brie, Yvette Nicole Brown, Gillian Jacobs & Megan Ganz Roundtable," *Daily Beast,* February 28, 2012, http://www.thedailybeast.com/articles/2012/02/28/community-alison-brie-yvette-nicole-brown-gillian-jacobs-megan-ganz-roundtable.html.
15 Quoted in Raymond, *Stars for Freedom,* 32.
16 Yuen, "Playing 'Ghetto,'" 239.
17 *Latinos Beyond Reel: Challenging a Media Stereotype,* directed by Miguel Picker and Chyng Sun (Northampton, MA: Media Education Foundation, 2012), DVD.
18 SAG-AFTRA. "Summary of the Agreement for the 2011 Screen Actors Guild Basic and Television Agreements and the 2011 AFTRA Exhibit A to the Network Television Code," http://www.sagaftra.org/files/sag/documents/2011_TV-Theatrical_Summary.pdf.
19 Lucy Liu, "A Woman as Sherlock's Dr. Watson Is 'Elementary,'" *Morning Edition,* National Public Radio, September 27, 2012.

20 *East of Main Street: Taking the Lead*, directed by Jonathan Yi (Home Box Office, 2015), DVD.

21 Samuel Jackson, Interview with Charlie Rose, *Charlie Rose*, Public Broadcasting System, July 30, 1998.

22 Jesse Washington, "Women and Minorities in Film: Latinas More Likely to Appear Nude in Movies, Study Says," Associated Press, August 4, 2014, http://www.scpr.org/news/2014/08/04/45759/hollywood-diversity-latinas-more-likely-to-appear/.

23 Ibid.

24 Looping is voicing the background characters in a given scene (e.g., restaurants, street scenes, parties).

25 Kristen J. Warner, "A Black Cast Doesn't Make a Black Show: CITY OF ANGELS and the Plausible Deniability of Color-Blindness," in *Watching While Black: Centering the Television of Black Audiences*, ed. Beretta E. Smith-Shomade (New Brunswick, NJ: Rutgers University Press, 2012), 55.

26 *East of Main Street*.

27 Angelica Jade Bastién, "The Case against Colorblind Casting," *Atlantic*, December 26, 2015, http://www.theatlantic.com/entertainment/archive/2015/12/oscar-isaac-and-the-case-against-colorblind-casting/421668/.

28 Sidney Poitier, "Oprah Talks to Sidney Poitier," *O*, October 2000, http://www.oprah.com/omagazine/Oprah-Interviews-Sidney-Poitier.

29 Antonio José Ríos-Bustamante, *Latinos in Hollywood* (Encino, CA: Floricanto Press, 1991), 3–4; Alicia Arrizon, *Latina Performance: Traversing the Stage* (Bloomington: Indiana University Press, 1999), 35.

30 Edward Sakamoto, "Anna May Wong and the Dragon-Lady Syndrome," *Los Angeles Times*, July 12, 1987, http://articles.latimes.com/1987-07-12/entertainment/ca-3279_1_dragon-lady.

31 Washington, "Women and Minorities in Film."

32 Ibid.

33 Josie Huang, "Emmys 2014: Little Diversity among Winners," Southern California Public Radio, August 26, 2014.

34 Heidi Parker, "'I'm Not a Super Sexy Latina': Jane the Virgin's Gina Rodriguez Explains Why Her Success in Hollywood Is Different from Stars Like Jennifer Lopez," *Daily Mail.com*, March 22, 2015, http://www.dailymail.co.uk/tvshowbiz/article-3006530/Gina-Rodriguez-explains-success-Hollywood-different-stars-like-Jennifer-Lopez.html.

35 Marilyn Yarbrough and Crystal Bennett, "Cassandra and the 'Sistahs': The Peculiar Treatment of African American Women in the Myth of Women as Liars," *Journal of Gender, Race & Justice* 3 (Spring 2000): 636.

36 Stacey Smith and Marc Choueiti, "Black Characters in Popular Film: Is the Key to Diversifying Cinematic Content Held in the Hand of the Black Director?" (Los Angeles: University of Southern Californa Annenberg School for Communication and Journalism, 2011), 2.

37 Felicia R. Lee, "The Weight Those Heels Carry," *New York Times*, April 26, 2013, http://www.nytimes.com/2013/04/28/movies/the-weight-those-heels-carry.html.

38 FOX News Latino, "Two Hispanic Actresses Take Lead Roles in Mainstream TV Shows This Fall," *FOX News Latino* (2014), http://latino.foxnews.com/latino/entertainment/2014/07/29/two-hispanic-actresses-take-lead-roles-in-mainstream-tv-shows-this-fall/.

39 Momo, "Maggie Q and Mekhi Phifer Talk Racial Typecasting in Hollywood," *CAAM Presents,* May 2, 2014, http://caamedia.org/blog/2014/05/02/maggie-q-and-mekhi-phifer-talk-racial-typecasting-in-hollywood/.

40 Gail Sullivan, "John Cho of 'Selfie': 'I Experienced Racism,'" *Washington Post,* October 9, 2014, https://www.washingtonpost.com/news/morning-mix/wp/2014/10/09/john-cho-of-selfie-wants-roles-outside-any-asian-stereotype-2/.

41 Schilling, "Native Actors Walk Off Set of Adam Sandler Movie."

42 Krigwa Players. *Krigwa Players Little Negro Theater,* ca. 1926. W. E. B. Du Bois Papers (MS 312). Special Collections and University Archives, University of Massachusetts Amherst Libraries, 134. Krigwa Players Little Negro Theater was one of the first panethnic theaters in the United States created about, by, for, and near African Americans.

43 Monica White Ndounou, *Shaping the Future of African American Film: Color-Coded Economics and the Story Behind the Numbers* (New Brunswick, NJ: Rutgers University Press, 2013), 62.

44 Negro Ensemble Company, Inc., "Alumni," http://necinc.org/alumni/.

45 Ndounou, *Shaping the Future of African American Film*, 62.

46 Nicolas Kanellos, "Hispanic Theatre in the United States: Post-War to the Present," *Latin American Theatre Review* 25, no. 2 (1992), 198.

47 Ibid.

48 East West Players, "About Us: History," East West Players, http://eastwestplayers.org/about-us/; Josephine Ding Lee, *Performing Asian America: Race and Ethnicity on the Contemporary Stage*, Asian American History and Culture (Philadelphia: Temple University Press, 1997).

49 The major studios are Walt Disney Studios Motion Pictures, Paramount Pictures Corporation, Sony Pictures Entertainment Inc., Twentieth Century Fox Film Corporation, Universal City Studios LLC, and Warner Bros. Entertainment Inc., see Motion Picture Association of America, "Theatrical Market Statistics 2014" (Washington, D.C.: Author, 2015), 21.

50 Griselda Nevarez, "Not Many Roles for Latino Actors in Hollywood," *Huffpost Latino Voices,* May 27, 2013, http://www.huffingtonpost.com/2013/05/27/roles-for-latino-actors-in-hollywood_n_3342031.html.

51 Chris Rock, "Chris Rock Pens Blistering Essay on Hollywood's Race Problem: 'It's a White Industry,'" *Hollywood Reporter,* December 12, 2014, http://www.hollywoodreporter.com/news/top-five-filmmaker-chris-rock-753223.

52 Jen Yamato, "'The Birth of a Nation': Meet Nate Parker, the Revolutionary Filmmaker behind the Sundance Smash," *Daily Beast,* January 28, 2016, http://www.thedailybeast.com/articles/2016/01/28/the-birth-of-a-nation-meet-nate-parker-the-revolutionary-filmmaker-behind-the-sundance-smash.html.

53 Michelle Lanz, "'The Birth of a Nation' Director Nate Parker: 'Nat Turner Used an Axe. My Axe Is a Camera,'" *The Frame*, January 27, 2016, http://www.scpr.org/programs/the-frame/2016/01/27/46087/the-birth-of-a-nation-director-nate-parker-nat-tur/.

54 UCLA Film and Television Archive, "'L.A. Rebellion: Creating a New Black Cinema'—Exhibition," UCLA Film and Television Archive, http://www.cinema.ucla.edu/la-rebellion/la-rebellion-creating-new-black-cinema; Berg, *Latino Images in Film*, 185–186; Jun Xing, *Asian America through the Lens: History, Representations, and Identity* (Walnut Creek, CA: AltaMira, 1998), 31–52.

55 Michael Ajakawe, Personal interview with Christine Acham. "Blacks in the Future Braving the Frontier of the Web Series," in *Watching While Black: Centering the Television of Black Audiences*, ed. Beretta E. Smith-Shomade (New Brunswick, NJ: Rutgers University Press, 2012), 66.

56 Robert Ito, "Asian American Actors Find a Home on Youtube," *Los Angeles Times*, June 22, 2012, http://articles.latimes.com/2012/jun/22/entertainment/la-ca-yomyomf-20120624.

57 "Top 100 YouTubers by Subscribed," *Socialblade.com*, February 6, 2016, .https://socialblade.com/youtube/top/100/mostsubscribed.

58 Barbara Pearson et al., "6 YouTubers Making More Money Than You," *USA Today*, February 25, 2015, http://www.usatoday.com/story/tech/2015/02/24/youtube-smosh-pewdiepie-jennamarbles-nigahiga-macbarbie07/23947527/.

59 Ibid.

60 Ibid.

61 Nielsen, "State of the Media: Advertising & Audiences Part 2: By Demographic" (New York: Author, 2012).

62 TiVo, "TiVo Survey Shows Millennials Embrace Both the Old and the New," February 20, 2014, http://pr.tivo.com/press-releases/tivo-survey-shows-millennials-embrace-both-the-old-and-the-new-nasdaq-tivo-1091496.

63 Variety Staff, "Survey: Youtube Stars More Popular Than Mainstream Celebs among U.S. Teens," *Variety*, August 5, 2014, http://variety.com/2014/digital/news/survey-youtube-stars-more-popular-than-mainstream-celebs-among-u-s-teens-1201275245/.

64 Lee Rainie, "Asian-Americans and Technology" (Washington, DC: Pew Internet & American Life Project, 2011), http://www.pewinternet.org/2011/01/06/asian-americans-and-technology/.

65 Nielsen, "State of the Asian American Consumer: Growing Market, Growing Impact" (New York: Author, 2012), 10.

66 Nielsen, "Asian Americans: Culturally Connected and Forging the Future" (New York: Author, 2015).

67 Itay Hod, "How Hollywood Actors' Twitter Followings Have Become as Important as Talent," *The Wrap*, March 10, 2015, http://www.thewrap.com/how-hollywood-actors-twitter-followings-have-become-as-important-as-talent/.

68 Nellie Andreeva, "HBO Developing Comedy Series from Larry Wilmore & Issa Rae to Star Rae," *Deadline Hollywood,* August 6, 2013, http://deadline.com/2013/08/hbo-developing-comedy-series-from-larry-wilmore-issa-rae-to-star-rae-557790/.

69 Lilly Workneh, "Shonda Rhimes, Ava Duvernay, and Other Badass Women Grace the Cover of *Essence*'s May Issue," *Huffington Post,* April 14, 2015, http://www.huffingtonpost.com/2015/04/14/essence-magazine-may-cove_n_7065428.html?ir=Media&ncid=tweetlnkushpmg00000021.

## CHAPTER 7 DIVERSIFYING HOLLYWOOD

1 Gabriel Arana, "The Unbearable Whiteness of Liberal Media," *American Prospect* (2014), http://prospect.org/article/unbearable-whiteness-liberal-media#.U3EuUIaHpZk.twitter; Joann Weiner, "Diversity Is Good. Why Doesn't Everyone Agree?" *Washington Post,* November 26, 2014, https://www.washingtonpost.com/blogs/she-the-people/wp/2014/11/26/diversity-is-good-why-doesnt-everyone-agree/.

2 Weiner, "Diversity Is Good. Why Doesn't Everyone Agree?"

3 Donald Bogle, *Toms, Coons, Mulattoes, Mammies, and Bucks: An Interpretive History of Blacks in American Films* (New York: Continuum, 2001), 15; NAACP Hollywood Bureau. "Out of Focus out of Sync Take 4," ed. Pamela Johnson (Baltimore, MD: National Association for the Advancement of Colored People, December 2008), http://action.naacp.org/page/-/NAACP%20OFOS%20Take4.pdf.

4 NAACP Hollywood Bureau, "Out of Focus out of Sync Take 4."

5 Ibid., 2.

6 Jill Watts, *Hattie McDaniel: Black Ambition, White Hollywood* (New York: Amistad, 2005), 138.

7 Ibid., 4.

8 Emilie Raymond, *Stars for Freedom: Hollywood, Black Celebrities, and the Civil Rights Movement* (Seattle: University of Washington Press, 2015), 235.

9 Angela Chia-yi Pao, *No Safe Spaces: Re-Casting Race, Ethnicity, and Nationality in American Theater.* Theater: Theory/Text/Performance (Ann Arbor: University of Michigan Press, 2010), 56.

10 Ibid., 61.

11 Greg Braxton, "A White, White World on TV's Fall Schedule," *Los Angeles Times,* May 28 1999, http://articles.latimes.com/1999/may/28/news/mn-41995.

12 Greg Braxton, "Groups Join to Protest Exclusion," *Los Angeles Times,* June 25, 1999, http://articles.latimes.com/1999/jun/25/entertainment/ca-49871; Greg Braxton, "NAACP Will Fight Network TV Lineups," *Los Angeles Times,* July 12, 1999, http://articles.latimes.com/1999/jul/12/news/mn-55184; Ray Bradford, Interview by author, Los Angeles, November 13, 2012, Digital recording; NAACP, "Media Diversity Projects," National

Association for the Advancement of Colored People, http://www.naacp.org/pages/hollywood-bureau-projects.

13 Leonard M. Baynes, "White Out: The Absence and Stereotyping of People of Color by the Broadcast Networks in Prime Time Entertainment Programming," *Arizona Law Review* 45 (2003): 2.

14 Ibid.

15 Ed Moy, "APAMC Announces New Co-Chairs and New Directions," *Examiner.com,* January 14, 2013, http://www.examiner.com/article/asian-pacific-american-media-coalition-announces-new-co-chairs-and-direction; Braxton, "Groups Join to Protest Exclusion."

16 Moy, "APAMC Announces New Co-Chairs and New Directions."

17 Baynes, "White Out."

18 Ray Bradford, Interview by author; NAACP, "Media Diversity Projects."

19 Baynes, "White Out."

20 Eric Deggans, "FOX Says Diversity Leads to Good Ratings and Better Business," National Public Radio (2013), http://www.npr.org/blogs/codeswitch/2013/11/13/244988218/fox-says-diversity-leads-to-good-ratings-and-better-business.

21 Ibid.

22 Bradford Evans, "Talking to Mike Schur About 'Parks and Rec,' 'Brooklyn Nine-Nine,' and Writing with Bill Murray," *Splitsider* (2013), http://splitsider.com/2013/09/talking-to-mike-schur-about-parks-and-rec-brooklyn-nine-nine-and-writing-with-bill-murray/.

23 Christian Cintron, "'Brooklyn Nine-Nine' and the Future of Diversity," *Hollywood* (2013), http://www.hollywood.com/news/tv/55038595/brooklyn-nine-nine-future-diversity.

24 Deggans, "FOX Says Diversity Leads to Good Ratings and Better Business."

25 Braxton, "NAACP Will Fight Network TV Lineups."

26 Nina Shen Rastogi, "Casting and Race: The Tricky Business of Writing Casting Notices," *Slate.com* (2012), http://www.slate.com/articles/arts/culturebox/2012/07/casting_and_race_the_tricky_business_of_writing_casting_notices.single.html.

27 Austin Siegemund-Broka, "CBS Execs Talk Plans to Increase Diversity: It's 'Our Most Important Issue,'" *Hollywood Reporter,* November 7, 2014, http://www.hollywoodreporter.com/news/cbs-execs-talk-plans-increase-747602.

28 Ibid.

29 Ibid.

30 Nellie Andreeva, "Pilots 2015: The Year of Ethnic Castings," *Deadline Hollywood,* March 24, 2015, http://deadline.com/2015/03/tv-pilots-ethnic-casting-trend-backlash-1201386511/.

31 U.S. Department of Justice, "The Communications Act of 1934, 47 U.S.C. § 151 Et Seq.," U.S. Department of Justice, Office of Justice Programs, https://it.ojp.gov/default.aspx?area=privacy&page=1288.

32 Alexandra Kalev, Frank Dobbin, and Erin Kelly, "Best Practices or Best Guesses? Diversity Management and the Remediation of Inequality," *American Sociological Review* 71 (2006): 590.

33 Baynes, "White Out," 3.
34 Ibid.
35 Kalev, Dobbin, and Kelly, "Best Practices or Best Guesses?" 590.
36 Lexi Alexander, "Of Fear and Fake Diversity," *Lexi Alexander,* January 3, 2016, http://www.lexi-alexander.com/blog/lexi-alexander/blog-2.
37 Stacy L. Smith, "Hey, Hollywood: It's Time to Adopt the NFL's Rooney Rule—for Women (Guest Column)," *Hollywood Reporter,* February 15, 2014; Spike Lee, Facebook Post, January 18, 2016, 5:07am, https://www.facebook.com/SpikeLee/posts/10153864871164819:0.
38 Kalev, Dobbin, and Kelly, "Best Practices or Best Guesses?" 590.
39 Rebecca Sun, "TV Diversity Programs: Launching Pad or Scarlet Letter?" *Hollywood Reporter,* October 15, 2015, http://www.hollywoodreporter.com/features/tv-diversity-programs-launching-pad-831880.
40 Ibid.
41 Ibid.
42 T. L. Stanley, "The Next Aaron Spelling? Showrunner Shonda Rhimes Is ABC's Queen of Prime Time," *Adweek,* June 3, 2014, http://www.adweek.com/news/television/next-aaron-spelling-showrunner-shonda-rhimes-abcs-queen-prime-time-158042.
43 Chris Rock, "Chris Rock Pens Blistering Essay on Hollywood's Race Problem: 'It's a White Industry,'" *Hollywood Reporter,* December 12, 2014, http://www.hollywoodreporter.com/news/top-five-filmmaker-chris-rock-753223.
44 Jennifer A. Richeson and Richard J. Nussbaum, "The Impact of Multiculturalism versus Color-Blindness on Racial Bias," *Journal of Experimental Social Psychology* 40 (2003): 417–423; Laurie A. Rudman, Richard D. Ashmore, and Melvin L. Gary, "'Unlearning' Automatic Biases: The Malleability of Implicit Prejudice and Stereotypes," *Journal of Personality and Social Psychology* 81 (2001): 856–868; Kalev, Dobbin, and Kelly, "Best Practices or Best Guesses?" 589–617.
45 Keith Kamisugi, "Can 'Hollywood' Transform the Way We Understand Race?," *Huffington Post* (May 25, 2011), http://www.huffingtonpost.com/keith-kamisugi/can-hollywood-transform-t_b_468845.html.
46 SAGindie, SAGindie Resources, http://www.sagindie.org/resources.
47 Adam Moore, Phone interview by author, Digital recording. Los Angeles, December 12, 2012.
48 Ibid.
49 Mike Hodge, "New York Division President's Letter," *New York Vocal Local: The Official E-Newsletter of the New York Division* (2011), http://www.sagaftra.org/new-york-division/newsletters/new-york-201109/new-york-201109.
50 Ibid.
51 Cicely Sharp and Timothy Jon Curry, "Black Americans in Popular Magazines: The Effects of Audience Characteristics and the Persistence of Stereotypes," *Sociological Focus* 29, no. 4 (1996): 311–324.
52 http://www.abctalentdevelopment.com/programs/programs_castings.html.

53 http://diversity.cbscorporation.com/page.php?id=24.

54 Scott Collins, "With #Oscarssowhite, CBS' Diversity Talent Showcase Crackles with Added Relevance," *Los Angeles Times*, January 25, 2016, http://www.latimes.com/entertainment/tv/la-et-st-cbs-diversity-showcase-20160125-story.html.

55 Ibid.

56 http://www.standupnbc.com/about.

57 http://www.nbcunitips.com/nbc-scene-showcase/.

58 http://capeusa.org.

59 CAPE, "Cape Casting Workshop at ABC–Congrats Cape Members on a Terrific Workshop!" CAPE, http://capeusa.org/cape-casting-workshop-at-abc-congrats-cape-members-on-a-terrific-workshop/.

60 http://seejane.org.

61 http://seejane.org/membership/salon-reel-vs-real-diversity-hollywood-influencers-screen-behind-scenes/.

62 http://www.nalip.org/.

63 http://www.naacpimageawards.net.

64 http://www.almaawards.com.

65 SAG-AFTRA. "SAG-AFTRA Announces American Scene Award Recipients," http://www.sagaftra.org/sag-aftra-announces-american-scene-award-recipients.

66 Frances Negron-Muntaner et al., "The Latino Media Gap: A Report on the State of Latinos in U.S. Media" (New York: The Center for the Study of Ethnicity and Race, Columbia University, 2014).

67 David Ng, "Spike Lee and Jada Pinkett Smith to Boycott Oscars; Academy Responds." *Los Angeles Times,* January 18, 2016, http://www.latimes.com/entertainment/movies/la-et-spike-lee-to-boycott-oscars-html-20160118-htmlstory.html.

68 Janice Min, "#OscarsSoWhite: Academy Chiefs Reveal Behind-the-Scenes Drama That Led to Historic Change (Exclusive)," *Hollywood Reporter,* January 27, 2016, http://www.hollywoodreporter.com/features/oscarssowhite-academy-chiefs-reveal-behind-859693.

69 Shelli Weinstein, "How 'Scandal' Paved the Way for ABC's Twitter-Based '#TGIT' Marketing Strategy," *Variety,* September 22, 2014, http://variety.com/2014/tv/news/scandal-twitter-shonda-rhimes-tgit-abc-shondaland-1201311282/.

70 Pamela McClintock, "Summer Box Office: How Movie Tracking Went Off the Rails," *Hollywood Reporter,* September 3, 2015, http://www.hollywoodreporter.com/news/summer-box-office-how-movie-819250.

71 Ibid.

72 Caitlin Dewey, "#Bringbackourgirls, #Kony2012, and the Complete, Divisive History of 'Hashtag Activism,'" *Washington Post,* May 8, 2014, https://www.washingtonpost.com/news/the-intersect/wp/2014/05/08/bringbackourgirls-kony2012-and-the-complete-divisive-history-of-hashtag-activism/.

73 Julia Craven, "Black Lives Matter Was Absent from the GOP Debate," *Huffington Post,* September 17, 2015, http://www.huffingtonpost.com/entry/black-lives-matter-gop-debate_55fad66de4b0fde8b0cd30a9?utm_hp_ref=black; Lindsey Weedston, "12 Hashtags That Changed the World in 2014," *Yes!*, December 19, 2014, http://www.yesmagazine.org/people-power/12-hashtags-that-changed-the-world-in-2014; Jamilah King, "#Blacklivesmatter: How Three Friends Turned a Spontaneous Facebook Post into a Global Phenomenon," *California Sunday Magazine,* March 1, 2015, https://stories.californiasunday.com/2015-03-01/black-lives-matter/.

74 Josie Huang, "#Cancelcolbert: Suey Park, the Activist Behind the Hashtag" (Southern California Public Radio, March 29, 2014), http://www.scpr.org/blogs/multiamerican/2014/03/29/16229/cancel-colbert-twitter-suey-park-hashtag.

75 Soraya Nadia McDonald, "Cameron Crowe Apologizes for Casting Emma Stone in Whitewashed 'Aloha,'" *Washington Post,* June 3, 2015, https://www.washingtonpost.com/news/arts-and-entertainment/wp/2015/06/03/cameron-crowe-apologizes-for-casting-emma-stone-in-whitewashed-aloha/; Michael Pearson, "Matt Damon Apologizes over 'Project Greenlight' and 'Whitesplaining,'" *CNN.com,* September 17, 2015, http://www.cnn.com/2015/09/17/entertainment/matt-damon-project-greenlight-apology.

76 Elizabeth Wagmeister, "Viola Davis on Women and Diversity: 'They Exist in Life, We Should See It on TV' (Video)," *Variety,* September 18, 2015, http://variety.com/2015/tv/news/viola-davis-emmy-how-to-get-away-with-murder-women-diversity-1201597083/.

# SELECTED BIBLIOGRAPHY

Baynes, Leonard M. "White Out: The Absence and Stereotyping of People of Color by the Broadcast Networks in Prime Time Entertainment Programming." *Arizona Law Review* 45 (2003): 293–369.

Berg, Charles Ramírez. *Latino Images in Film: Stereotypes, Subversion, Resistance.* Austin: University of Texas Press, 2002.

Bogle, Donald. *Toms, Coons, Mulattoes, Mammies, and Bucks: An Interpretive History of Blacks in American Films.* New York: Continuum, 2001.

Bonilla-Silva, Eduardo. *Racism without Racists: Color-Blind Racism and the Persistence of Racial Inequality in the United States.* 2nd ed. Lanham, MD: Rowman & Littlefield Publishers, 2006.

Chin, Christina, Meera Deo, Jenny Lee, Noriko Milman, and Nancy Wang Yuen. "Asian Pacific Americans in Prime Time: Setting the Stage." Washington DC: Asian American Justice Center, 2006.

Directors Guild of America. "DGA TV Diversity Report: Employer Hiring of Women Directors Shows Modest Improvement; Women and Minorities Continue to Be Excluded in First-Time Hiring." http://www.dga.org/News/PressReleases/2015/150825-Episodic-Director-Diversity-Report.aspx.

———. "Employers Make No Improvement in Diversity Hiring in Episodic Television: DGA Report." 2014. http://www.dga.org/News/PressReleases/2014/140917-Episodic-Director-Diversity-Report.aspx.

*East of Main Street: Taking the Lead.* Directed by Jonathan Yi. Home Box Office, 2015. DVD.

Entman, Robert M., and Andrew Rojecki. *The Black Image in the White Mind: Media and Race in America.* Studies in Communication, Media, and Public Opinion. Chicago: University of Chicago Press, 2000.

Eschholz, Sarah, Ted Chiricos, and Marc Gertz, "Television and Fear of Crime: Program Types, Audience Traits, and the Mediating Effect of Perceived Neighborhood Racial Composition." *Social Problems* 50, no. 3 (2003): 395–415.

Feagin, Joe R. *Racist America: Roots, Current Realities, and Future Reparations.* New York: Routledge, 2000.

Federal Communications Commission. "Report on Ownership of Commercial Broadcast Stations." Washington, DC: Federal Communications Commission, 2014.

Hall, Stuart. "Culture, Media, and the 'Ideological Effect.'" In *Mass Communication and Society,* edited by J. Curran, M. Gurevitch, and J. Woollacott, 315–348. London: Edward Arnold, 1977.

Horn, John, and Doug Smith, "Diversity Efforts Slow to Change the Face of Oscar Voters." *Los Angeles Times,* December 21, 2013. http://www.latimes.com/entertainment/movies/moviesnow/la-et-mn-diversity-oscar-academy-members-20131221-story.html.

Hunt, Darnell, and Ana-Christina Ramon. "2015 Hollywood Diversity Report: Flipping the Script." Los Angeles: Ralph J. Bunche Center for African American Studies at UCLA, 2015.

Hunt, Darnell, Ana-Christina Ramon, and Michael Tran. "2016 Hollywood Diversity Report: Busine$$ as Usual?" Los Angeles: Ralph J. Bunche Center for African American Studies at UCLA, 2016.

Lauzen, Martha M. "It's a Man's (Celluloid) World: On-Screen Representations of Female Characters in the Top 100 Films of 2013." San Diego: San Diego State University, Center for the Study of Women in Television and Film, 2014.

Lee, Joann Faung Jean. *Asian American Actors: Oral Histories from Stage, Screen, and Television.* Jefferson, NC: McFarland, 2000.

Lee, Robert G., *Orientals: Asian Americans in Popular Culture.* Philadelphia: Temple University Press, 1999.

Ndounou, Monica White. *Shaping the Future of African American Film: Color-Coded Economics and the Story behind the Numbers.* New Brunswick, NJ: Rutgers University Press, 2013.

Neely, Priska, "To Avoid or to Embrace? How Actors Navigate Stereotypes." *Talk of the Nation:* National Public Radio, May 1, 2013.

Negron-Muntaner, Frances, Chelsea Abbas, Luis Figueroa, and Samuel Robson. "The Latino Media Gap: A Report on the State of Latinos in U.S. Media." New York: Columbia University, Center for the Study of Ethnicity and Race, 2014.

Pachon, Harry P., Louis DeSipio, Rodolfo O. de la Garza, and Chon Noriega. "Missing in Action: Latinos in and out of Hollywood." Edited by Patrick Lee and Joy Hofer. Claremont, CA: The Tomas Rivera Policy Institute, 1999.

Quinn, Eithne. "Closing Doors: Hollywood, Affirmative Action, and the Revitalization of Conservative Racial Politics." *Journal of American History* 99, no. 2 (2012): 466–491.

Raymond, Emilie. *Stars for Freedom: Hollywood, Black Celebrities, and the Civil Rights Movement.* Seattle: University of Washington Press, 2015.

Robinson, Russell. "Casting and Caste-ing: Reconciling Artistic Freedom and Antidiscrimination Norms." *California Law Review* 95, no. 1 (February 2007): 1–73.

Robinson, Russell, Su Li, Angela Makabali, and Kaitlyn Murphy. "Not Quite a Breakthrough: The Oscars and Actors of Color, 2002–2012." *Latino Policy & Issues Brief*, edited by Chon A. Noriega, 4. Los Angeles: UCLA Chicano Studies Research Center, 2012.

Rock, Chris. "Chris Rock Pens Blistering Essay on Hollywood's Race Problem: 'It's a White Industry.'" *Hollywood Reporter*, December 12, 2014. http://www.hollywoodreporter.com/news/top-five-filmmaker-chris-rock-753223.

Ryzik, Melena. "What It's Really Like to Work in Hollywood* (*If You're Not a Straight White Man.)." *New York Times*, February 24, 2016, http://www.nytimes.com/interactive/2016/02/24/arts/hollywood-diversity-inclusion.html?smid=fb-nytimes&smtyp=cur&_r=0.

Smith, Stacey, and Marc Choueiti. "Black Characters in Popular Film: Is the Key to Diversifying Cinematic Content Held in the Hand of the Black Director?" Los Angeles: University of Southern California Annenberg School for Communication and Journalism, 2011.

Smith, Stacey, Marc Choueiti, and Katherine Pieper. "Media, Diversity, & Social Change Initiative," 27. Los Angeles: Institute for Diversity and Empowerment at Annenberg (IDEA), 2016.

———. "Race/Ethnicity in 600 Popular Films: Examining on Screen Portrayals and Behind-the-Camera Diversity." *Media, Diversity, and Social Change Initiative*. Los Angeles: University of Southern California Annenberg School for Communication and Journalism, 2014.

Timberlake, Jeffrey M., Junia Howell, Amy Baumann Grau, and Rhys H. Williams. "Who 'They' Are Matters: Immigrant Stereotypes and Assessments of the Impact of Immigration." *Social Science Quarterly* 56, no. 2 (2015): 267–299.

Watts, Jill. *Hattie McDaniel: Black Ambition, White Hollywood*. New York: Amistad, 2005.

Weaver, Andrew J. "The Role of Actors' Race in White Audiences' Selective Exposure to Movies." *Journal of Communication* 61 (2011): 369–385.

Weisbuch, Max, Kristin Pauker, and Nalini Ambady. "The Subtle Transmission of Race Bias via Televised Nonverbal Behavior." *Science* 326 (December 18, 2009): 1711–1714.

Xing, Jun. *Asian America through the Lens: History, Representations, and Identity*. Walnut Creek, CA: AltaMira, 1998.

Yuen, Nancy Wang. "Actors, Asian American." In *Asian American Society: An Encyclopedia*, ed. Mary Yu Danico, 18–22. Thousand Oaks, CA: Sage, 2014.

———. "Performing Race, Negotiating Identity: Asian American Professional Actors in Hollywood." In *Asian American Youth Culture, Identity, and Ethnicity*, ed. Jennifer Lee and Min Zhou, 251–267. New York: Routledge, 2004.

———. "Playing 'Ghetto': Black Actors, Stereotypes, and Authenticity." In *Black Los Angeles: American Dreams and Racial Realities*, edited by Darnell Hunt and Ana-Christina Ramon, 232–242. New York: New York University Press, 2010.

Yuen, Nancy Wang, Christina Chin, Meera Deo, Jenny Lee, and Noriko Milman. "Asian Pacific Americans in Prime Time: Lights, Camera, and Little Action." Washington, DC: National Asian Pacific American Legal Consortium, 2005.

# INDEX

Page numbers in *italics* refer to figures or tables.

# ABOUT THE AUTHOR

NANCY WANG YUEN is an associate professor of sociology at Biola University. Yuen earned her undergraduate degree in English with a specialization in creative writing poetry and her doctorate degree in sociology at the University of California at Los Angeles. Yuen produced the documentary *Mass Confucian: Chinese Language or Propaganda?* and is curating a museum exhibit on Hollywood's Pioneering Asian American actresses.